Twelve Virtues

"Throughout this delightful book of sermons, Craig Mindrum brings to the Scriptures all the tools of modern biblical criticism and then crafts sermons that are profound, faithful, pastoral, and as timely as the daily newspaper. Mindrum's aim is 'not a dismantling of faith, but a deepening of it,' as he states in his introduction. I commend these erudite sermons for personal devotional use or group study and discussion. Most likely, they will provoke lively conversation."

—**ALBERT G. BUTZER III,**
Retired Clergy, Presbyterian Church (USA), Norfolk, Virginia

"Craig Mindrum has here gifted us with a fresh and creative approach to biblical interpretation in the service of preaching. He invites us to bring responsible scholarly interpretation into practical engagement with challenges of faithful living in our time. The chapters demonstrate how that is possible and why it is essential. Mindrum's writing is prophetic and profoundly insightful. It is spiced with humor and down-to-earth grappling with real-life issues. The book is commendably accessible and will prove usable for devotional reading, small group discussions, and for pastors as an aid to more faithful and effective preaching."

—**ANNA CASE-WINTERS,**
Professor of Theology, McCormick Theological Seminary, Chicago

"Before sermons emerge in the preaching moment, they must first crack open new life and space in the preacher. The most powerful sermons come from the wrestling of the one giving the sermon—wrestling with the text, the historical context, our own complicated experiences, our honest questions, communities searching for a way forward, and even with God's own self. One of the gifts of this collection of sermons is permission—permission to wrestle with hard questions, serious scholarship, and counter the rising tide of Christian nationalism. What begins to emerge on these pages are examples of sermons that model a different kind of Christianity—one that gives permission to center the virtues that mirror what we pray when we plead, 'Thy kingdom come, thy will be done, on earth as it is in heaven.'"

—**TROY E. MEDLIN,**
Associate Pastor, Grace Lutheran Church and School,
River Forest, Illinois

Twelve Virtues

Sermons That Unite Honest Scholarship with the Good News of a Living Faith

CRAIG MINDRUM

Foreword by Albert G. Butzer III

RESOURCE *Publications* · Eugene, Oregon

TWELVE VIRTUES
Sermons That Unite Honest Scholarship with the Good News of a Living Faith

Resource Publications
An Imprint of Wipf and Stock Publishers
199 W. 8th Ave., Suite 3
Eugene, OR 97401

www.wipfandstock.com

PAPERBACK ISBN: 979-8-3852-6243-4
HARDCOVER ISBN: 979-8-3852-6244-1
EBOOK ISBN: 979-8-3852-6245-8

VERSION NUMBER 03/24/26

For Danuta M. Mindrum, Jennifer K. Mindrum, Jessica C. Mindrum
. . . and the late Jonathan C. Mindrum (1987-2024).
We will love you forever.

"Let all that you do be done in love."

—1 Cor 16:14 (NRSV)

CONTENTS

Foreword

It is God himself, in his mercy, who has given us this wonderful work [of telling the Good News to others], and so we never give up. We do not try to trick people into believing—we are not interested in fooling anyone. We never try to get anyone to believe that the Bible teaches what it doesn't. All such shameful methods we forego. We stand in the presence of God as we speak and so we tell the truth, as all who know us will agree. . . . We don't go around preaching about ourselves, but about Jesus Christ as Lord.

—2 Cor 4:1-2, 5 TLB

As a first-year seminary student, I enrolled in a class called "Introduction to the Old Testament." One day the professor lectured about Exodus and told us that the biblical words "Red Sea" are more accurately translated "Sea of Reeds," suggesting something like a shallow, marshy body of water.

My seminary roommate and I had very different reactions to this idea. I loved it! For me the professor's suggestion was eye-opening and intellectually freeing, allowing me to imagine a faithful alternative to the enormous wall of water pictured quite dramatically in Cecil B. DeMille's classic movie, *The Ten Commandments*. After all, I said to myself, the point of the story is not so much how the people of Israel crossed the water, but that God delivered them from bondage in Egypt to freedom in the desert.

My roommate felt differently. He came from a conservative church upbringing and brought to seminary a literal or fundamentalist reading of Scripture. He found the words "Sea of Reeds" to be unsettling, unorthodox, and a challenge to his faith. Not surprisingly, he withdrew from the seminary after the first semester and transferred to a school that taught the Bible the way he thought it should be taught.

Here, then, are two very different ways to read and interpret the Bible. For my roommate, the Bible is a book to be revered as God's holy and immutable word. People should accept it without questioning, for questioning can lead to doubt, and doubt to a faltering faith. My roommate might well have adhered to the bumper sticker words that Craig Mindrum warns against in one of his sermons: "God said it. I believe it. That settles it."

On the other hand, the professor approached the Scriptures using the modern tools of biblical criticism, a method of study that examines the Bible from a variety of viewpoints: cultural, historical, archaeological, and linguistic, to name a few. One of my denomination's statements of faith, "The Confession of 1967," describes this approach with these words: "The Scriptures, given under the guidance of the Holy Spirit, are nevertheless words of human beings," and urges people to regard the Scriptures "with literary and historic understanding."[1]

Another way to think about biblical criticism is in terms of something that has been called "The Interpreter's Triangle." Imagine an equilateral triangle where each corner stands for something different. One corner represents the biblical text itself. What does the text say? What is its plain meaning? The second corner represents the context in which the text was originally written. What was going on when the text was written—historically, culturally, linguistically, pre-scientifically? What were the author's experiences, biases? The third corner of the triangle represents the context is which the text is being read. What assumptions does the reader/interpreter bring to the present moment, historical, cultural, scientific, political, etc.? It goes without saying that reading a text

1. "Confession of 1967," *The Book of Confessions*, Section 9.29, p. 291.

today can lead us to a very different interpretation than reading it in 1000 or 1600 or even 2026 A.D. Consider, for example, how our views have changed over the course of time concerning ideas like the role of women in society, dietary restrictions (God says, "Don't eat lobster"), science, ethics, slavery, divorce, and the place of gays and lesbians in church and culture.

Throughout this delightful book of sermons, Craig Mindrum brings to the Scriptures all the tools of modern Biblical criticism and then crafts sermons that are profound, faithful, pastoral, and as timely as the daily newspaper. Current events are never far from his thinking. Nor are the needs of those whom society has marginalized. Nor are the day-to-day concerns of everyday people. He draws insights from poets, philosophers, social critics, historians, and theologians and insists that these non-biblical voices enrich and clarify our understanding of the ancient Biblical texts. He uses metaphors, images, and anecdotes with care and precision. He discusses themes such as love, uncertainty, courage, forgiveness, and trust in ways I found helpful.

In each of these sermons, Craig's aim is "not a dismantling of faith, but a deepening of it," as he states in his introduction. Indeed, the words from *The Living Bible* which appear at the beginning of this preface might well serve as a partial motive for Craig's approach to preaching:

> We do not try to trick people into believing—we are not interested in fooling anyone. We never try to get anyone to believe that the Bible teaches what it doesn't. All such shameful methods we forego.

I commend these erudite sermons for personal devotional use or group study and discussion. Most likely, they will provoke lively conversation.

In my retirement, I spend a lot of time with my camera as well as reading books to help me become a better photographer. Recently, I came across an essay which addresses the mindset that photographers can bring to their craft. It refers to the paradoxical Zen Buddhist concepts of "no-mind" and "not knowing."

In the state of not knowing, we strive to suspend our fixed judgments and preconceptions. We maintain a healthy curiosity and attentive interest to the ever-changing here and now. New, creative discoveries cannot be made in a mind overfilled with opinions and speculations. Instead, the mind can be open and can cultivate an enthusiastic, child-like wonder. The mind inquires rather than thinks it knows. Active questioning forms the ideal creative working state.

It seems to me that these wise words written for photographers apply equally to Craig Mindrum's excellent sermons. If readers approach the Scriptures with their minds already made up, saying something like, "I already know what these ancient words mean," then they may miss out on any new word from the Lord. But if readers can approach the Scriptures with Zen-like open minds and child-like wonder, then these sermons will guide them to new truths and deeper faith in Christ and the Scriptures which bear witness to him.

On a personal note, Craig and I first met in the late 1980s when he and his family became members of the church I was serving at the time. Although I was called away from that church in 1994, we have remained friends these many years. He is one of the few people with whom I can talk about most anything, but especially about topics like the Bible, faith, and Christian theology. Most every time we speak or trade emails, he brings profound insights to our conversations. I am honored to write this foreword for his book.

The Reverend Albert G. Butzer III
Retired Clergy, Presbyterian Church (USA)
Norfolk, Virginia

Introduction

THE SERMONS IN THIS book are teaching sermons in that they aim not just to inspire, but to clarify what we can responsibly claim about Jesus, scripture, and faith in light of historical-critical scholarship. Such analysis is a way of studying the Bible that looks at who wrote it, when and where it was written, and what it meant in its own time. Instead of just assuming everything is literal or directly from God, it accommodates the history and culture behind the text to better understand its original intent, how it has been interpreted through time, and what it can mean for today.

These are not teaching sermons in the sense of dry lectures, but in the sense of seeking contemporary truthfulness when we take the best of modern scholarship seriously. Scholarship is in the background throughout, not the foreground, avoiding a mere academic focus.

The twelve sermons correspond to "big ideas" in the evolution of human thought, especially in a Christian context. They are virtues in the broadest sense. Some sermons refer to classic virtues of the Church—the theological virtues of faith, hope, and love, and the cardinal virtues of wisdom, justice, and courage. Other big ideas explored include learning, knowledge, freedom, joy, judgment, and repentance/forgiveness.

Each asks, what do these virtues mean if we are candid about what the gospels do and do not preserve from Jesus himself? My aim is to speak with clarity, reverence, and pastoral imagination, offering not a dismantling of faith but a deepening of it. I believe that truth, faced directly, is not the enemy of faith but its most necessary companion. Scholarship should be used as a tool for faith, not as a hammer against it.

My hope is that these sermons might serve as monthly devotionals for Christians and others interested in religious reflections. They are meant to inspire, instruct, and provoke thoughtful engagement with scripture—always with clarity, reverence, and pastoral imagination.

The Craft of Preaching

Historical-critical preaching carries risks. At its worst, it can become overly academic, heavy with detail, and inattentive to the heart. I have heard such sermons, and they deserve their oblivion. But I have also heard shallow sermons that avoid scholarship altogether, leaving hearers with little more than plain readings and pious platitudes. Neither extreme is sufficient.

Walter Brueggemann, in the preface to his *Collected Sermons*, writes that "the biblical text itself . . . is an act of imagination not much illuminated by historical-critical study of the kind fostered by the Jesus Seminar."[2]

He is surely right to insist that preaching must engage imagination, not only information. Yet why should imagination and historical-critical scholarship necessarily be opposed? Too often, bad preaching arises when academic insight cannot be translated into the lived poetry of a sermon. But that is not the only possibility. When scholarship is carried with pastoral imagination, it does not stifle the text but rather enlarges it.

As Brueggemann also insists, "The work of the sermon is to make the biblical text available to the church, so that church folk can, if they choose, reimagine their lives according to the strange cadences of the text."[3]

Historical-critical scholarship, when used with imagination—and not forced on people but used as an ever-present background

2. Brueggemann, *Collected Sermons*, 9.

3. Brueggemann, *Collected Sermons*, 11.

presence—can make scripture more available, not less. Far from closing the text down, it can open it wider.

The Church in Crisis

My own scholarly perspective is an expression of a long theological tradition that arose after the Enlightenment of the seventeenth century, when reason, science, and a historical perspective were introduced to the study and practice of religion. This tradition came to be known in many quarters eventually as "liberal theology"—theology freed from the constraints of biblical literalism and an antiscientific view of the world.

But liberal theology today lives in a difficult in-between: too academic and secular for some, too religious for others. Books rooted in liberal theology continue to be written, yet attendance at more liberal churches keeps dwindling. Ideas abound, but inspiration falters.

Therefore, the marriage of proclamation and scholarship found in this book is not only possible but may also be necessary. What if the problem is not that theology has gone too deep, but that preaching has not gone deep enough? Might congregations be more nourished by sermons that are honest about the text, yet also bold in showing how faith can speak to the urgent needs of our world? What if critical scholarship, far from emptying the sanctuary, could actually help refill it—by giving people words they can trust, and a vision they can live?

In the Tradition of Preaching

In terms of preaching, I also work from a long and extensive precedent. The teaching sermon has been part of Christian practice for many years, especially among Protestants. John Wesley's sermons sought to unite reason, scripture, and lived experience. Harry Emerson Fosdick, standing in Riverside Church, modeled what he called "preaching as counseling," addressing real human struggles while drawing on careful study. Paul Tillich preached with philosophical depth; Marcus Borg and John Dominic Crossan bring historical rigor to the church and its proclamations. Each, in their way, has joined scholarship to proclamation. I also owe much to Fred Craddock, Barbara Brown Taylor, and David Buttrick.

The sermons collected here belong in that lineage. They are not lectures dressed up as homilies, nor pieties wrapped in scriptural quotations. They are attempts to let the ancient text speak honestly, critically, and imaginatively—to faith and to the world we inhabit now.

We are all part of an evolving conversation. One important guiding principle in this conversation is that, whatever interpretive differences arise, everything we do must be done in love (1 Cor 16:14).

Suggested Further Reading

1. Fred B. Craddock, *As One Without Authority.* A classic on narrative and inductive preaching, emphasizing listening to the text rather than imposing on it.
2. Walter Brueggemann, *The Prophetic Imagination.* Shows how scholarship illuminates scripture while challenging conventional interpretations.
3. Barbara Brown Taylor, *The Preaching Life.* Models the integration of story, scholarship, and pastoral voice.
4. David L. Buttrick, *Homiletic: Moves and Structures.* A technical yet readable guide to sermon form and how structure shapes meaning.
5. Marcus J. Borg, *Speaking Christian.* Introduces historical-critical insights into the life and words of Jesus in a readable, accessible way. Also see *The Heart of Christianity.*
6. John Dominic Crossan, *The Historical Jesus: The Life of a Mediterranean Jewish Peasant.* Scholarly but influential in bridging academic research with public teaching.

7. Paul Tillich, *The Shaking of the Foundations* (Sermons). Preaching that models intellectual rigor married to pastoral sensitivity.

A Note on the Text

I have not been overly concerned about harmonizing the style and voice of the sermons. Some will read as sermonic essays; others will read as if preached. For the latter, I have often used an oral rhetorical style, and sometimes have included a few instructions just as I gave them during the sermon. For example, "Follow along with me in the bulletin." This can give readers a sense of the experience of being in the pews. Each sermon emerged with its own distinctive voice, and I have just run with that.

I have also not tried to harmonize the length of the sermons. Some seem just the right length. Others are on the longish side. A couple of them are overlong. Here again, though, I have (within reason) let them be what they wanted to be.

A Note on Terms

Throughout this book I use the term "Hebrew Bible" to refer to what Christians traditionally call the Old Testament. I make this choice out of respect for Jewish tradition and for clarity.

JANUARY

Learning

"Trying to Make Sense"

S.PAVLVS
I.° EREMIT.A
IO.
Israel ex.
IANVA

LEARNING: *"Trying to Make Sense"*

MATT 9: 10–13

And as he sat at dinner in the house, many tax collectors and sinners came and were sitting with Jesus and his disciples. When the Pharisees saw this, they said to his disciples, "Why does your teacher eat with tax collectors and sinners?" But when he heard this, he said, "Those who are well have no need of a physician, but those who are sick. Go and learn what this means, 'I desire mercy, not sacrifice.' For I have not come to call the righteous but sinners." (NRSV)

PHIL 4: 8–9

Finally, brothers and sisters, whatever is true, whatever is honorable, whatever is just, whatever is pure, whatever is pleasing, whatever is commendable, if there is any excellence and if there is anything worthy of praise, think about these things. As for the things that you have learned and received and heard and noticed in me, do them, and the God of peace will be with you. (NRSV)

I WANT TO TALK TODAY about the place of learning or education in our faith, our faith development, and our use of scripture. I am writing this for the beginning of the calendar year because this seems a good time to set the ground rules for how scripture will be used and interpreted throughout the rest of this series.

Here is a true story from my past. In an education class in college, our teacher asked us to draw a picture of what we thought learning was like. I drew a very large pitcher of water, in front of which were successively smaller jars and cups. A picture, I guess, of receiving "the truth" and then pouring it into others as received. I blush to admit that I served as a perfect foil for the teacher that day because another student drew an electrical tower connected to many other electrical towers. (Today, these would be cell towers and mobile phones.) Yes, we all agreed. That was right. Mine was . . . not so right.

My main point in this sermon is that I want to capture that sense of electricity in learning about Jesus and the church. Not an education we receive passively, but an education in which we participate actively. I want us wrestling with scripture and other writers. I want us to embrace uncertainty as one legitimate path to learning.

The word "learning" in the Hebrew Bible is largely a matter of learning about received dogma—learn to fear the Lord, learn his commandments, learn his law, learn his precepts. A similar example from the Christian New Testament has Paul cautioning the Romans not to succumb to those preaching against the doctrine they have learned. And in his letter to the Philippians, Paul says, "What you have learned and received and heard and seen in me, do [that]."

What's the main theme, then, of this understanding of "learning"? It's that God has given you the truth, whole and indisputable, and your job now is to learn enough so that you understand this truth better.

For thousands of Bible studies across the country, and maybe around the world, I suspect that this is the main thrust. Here is God's perfect word. Now the burden is on us to enlarge our minds enough to understand. If we believe there is something false or damaging in the text, well, the fault lies with us, not with the text. We are not learning well enough, or we are resisting the truth.

I have two types of concerns about this mindset. One is that I think it leaves young adults, especially, unprepared for what they are going to learn as they grow older. If we teach them only a closed-in biblical worldview, they will learn rather quickly of other understandings of human beings and their place in the universe. They will study science, sociology, and psychology. Possibly they will study theology and the Bible from a broader historical perspective or learn of other world religions. What happens then?

The danger is that they may decide that everything they've been taught is simply untrue. "You mean the world wasn't *actually* created in six days? You mean Jesus didn't *actually* walk on water? How many other things have you been telling me that aren't true?" And they may just throw the whole thing out—this whole religion business. And we may lose them forever.

I am thinking here of the effect of false statements on a number of kinds of groups. For example, the "ex-evangelicals" about whom Christian historian and author Diana Butler Bass writes—kids thrown out from or who left a fundamentalist, literalist church. She speaks of "the people, the human beings who were treated as litter by evangelical leaders and institutions on a crusade for religious, social, and political power, a quest that wrecked their souls and their sanity."[1]

This brings up a second concern. As your children grow and learn, and perhaps become supporters of things like LGBTQ rights, concern for the environment, and concern for racial and economic justice, they may not be as prepared as they need to be for attacks from far-right fundamentalist-literalists—those with a basic, simplistic theology and who interpret the Bible literally and as infallible, without error. Such people and their sects will throw Bible verses out of context at your children, and kids need enough learning to counter the attacks.

So much cruelty and misinformation are foisted upon people by a literal reading of scripture—the belief that "such and such" *really happened* or was *really said* just as written. You can defend yourself and your family against that misuse of scripture by "defanging" it, I call it, so it can't do as much damage. Let's consider

1. Butler Bass, Diana. "Evangelical Wreckage," *The Cottage*, October 19, 2022.

both the Hebrew Bible (mostly as interpreted by Christians) and the Christian New Testament.

First, the phrase "the Bible" is without much special meaning. It just means a collection of books. Saying, "Read the Bible" is like saying, "Read the Chicago Public Library." You can teach your kids how to defend themselves against people who say that something is "in the Bible." The first response can be, "Which particular book in the Bible are you talking about?"

One essential part of protecting your kids (and yourself) involves seeing the hand of human authorship in scripture. I well recall when I got far enough along in my education to learn "higher criticism" or "historical criticism" (as it is called) so that I could understand how different books of the Bible were written and put together by ancient people.

Some sects of the global Christian church affirm this kind of learning. In the Presbyterian Church U.S.A., for example, one of their confessions (the Confession of 1967) reads, "The Bible is to be interpreted in the light of its witness to God's work of reconciliation in Christ. The Scriptures, given under the guidance of the Holy Spirit, are nevertheless words of human beings." They are "conditioned by the language, thought forms, and literary fashions of the places and times at which they were written." They "reflect views of life, history, and the cosmos which were then current. The church, therefore, has an obligation to approach the Scriptures with literary and historical understanding."[2]

That is, they are a product of their time and what people understood about the world back then. To those writing at about the time of Jesus, the earth was the center of the universe. So we wouldn't trust scripture for astronomical insights, right? Diseases were caused by people's sins, not by bacteria and viruses, so we wouldn't trust scripture for medical advice.

How freeing that is—not reading the Bible as perfect and error-free, but trying to understand the people at the time the stories were written and what they knew and cared about. What wonderful rooms of interpretation and understanding are opened

2. "Confession of 1967," *The Book of Confessions*, Section 9.29, p. 291.

to us by learning how scriptural stories went from oral to written to edited to rewritten and on and on—how they were influenced by historical events and scientific beliefs at the time they were written. What insights into human thinking and the human condition are made available to us!

To counter the claim by some sects of Christianity that scripture is "infallible" (that is, without error), it's important to understand and learn just a little bit about the hand of authorship in scripture—seeing the mindsets of those human beings who wrote the Bible. I think even young kids—say, middle school and up—can get this point. Here's one example: In the Genesis creation story, were humans created first, and then the animals? Or was it animals first, then humans? It has to be one or the other, right? The answer is that both options are in Genesis. Two different ancient religious traditions with two different stories were mashed together.

See? Recognizing the hand of authorship. Again, it is very freeing. Like opening a cell door.

Importantly, Jesus used the concept of learning in a different way than simply receiving dogma unquestioningly. In our reading for today from Matthew, Jesus explains his ministry to outcasts and sinners: "Go and learn what this means, 'I desire mercy and not sacrifice'" (a line from the book of Hosea in the Hebrew Bible). See the difference? You are an independent mind. Don't just sit there. Go learn.

Some of you may feel apprehension about this approach to learning. If I start to take this historical view of scripture, will my faith suffer? I understand this to be more than a small concern. But see, that's evidence of the whole problem. My faith, your faith, does not depend on whether any particular story in the Bible is literally true. We need to learn, we need to educate ourselves so that people cannot hurt us with their corrupted views of scripture, which they will wield as a weapon. Scripture contains many examples of beauty and wisdom. It also contains unspeakably cruel and false things. The Bible is a record of imperfect human beings *trying to figure things out*, trying to learn—trying to make sense of the world and the cosmos. Sometimes they got it right, sometimes they got it partly right, and sometimes they got it just plain, grievously wrong.

Learning to see and understand in scripture what's helpful and strengthening to us, and what's not, needs to be part of your learning process, and your kids', and therefore how you provide learning experiences about religion in your home.

I am optimistic about this—about helping our children learn so they know enough to care about our faith, and especially about how Jesus revolutionized our relationship with God, and also taught us the importance of caring for the poor, the sick, the needy, the suffering, and the outcast. I am optimistic that this is a recipe for retaining our children in the church into their adult lives.

Our God, help us learn how to learn—how to learn in a way that ennobles us, and helps all of us to grow and stretch ourselves in service to the Church and the world.

Amen.

FEBRUARY

Love

"Jesus, Looking at Him, Loved Him"

TRĀS. S. AVGVSTI:
NI. EPĪ

Israel ex.

28. feb

Love: *"Jesus, Looking at Him, Loved Him"*

Mark 10: 17–22

As he was setting out on a journey, a man ran up and knelt before him and asked him, "Good Teacher, what must I do to inherit eternal life?" Jesus said to him, . . . "You know the commandments: 'You shall not murder. You shall not commit adultery. You shall not steal. You shall not bear false witness. You shall not defraud. Honor your father and mother.'" He said to him, "Teacher, I have kept all these since my youth." Jesus, looking at him, loved him and said, "You lack one thing; go, sell what you own, and give the money to the poor, and you will have treasure in heaven; then come, follow me." When he heard this, he was shocked and went away grieving, for he had many possessions. (NRSV)

W*ell, the greeting cards, flowers, and candy* now sit prominently in stores, and TV ads for jewelry are proliferating. Valentine's Day must almost be here!

I am poking just mild fun here, as I count myself among those who once took this day fairly seriously. Nice dinners, flowers, jewelry, you name it. Until about a decade ago when my wife and I just earnestly asked each other, "Can we not make a big deal about Valentine's Day? No gifts. Maybe make a dinner at home and watch a movie?"

There's a lesson here about older love needing less constant affirmation than a younger one, but that's a sermon for another time. Right now, it's February. Let's talk about love.

Are you surprised at the New Testament text I chose to anchor this sermon? Perhaps. A sermon on love might be expected to focus primarily on the beautiful hymn to love in Paul's first letter to the Corinthian church. Some of you know the lines well: "If I speak in the tongues of mortals and of angels, but do not have love, I am no more than a noisy gong or a clanging cymbal."

First Corinthians 13 is arguably the best description of the essentials of love ever written: Love is patient and kind; it is not jealous or boastful; it does not insist on its own way; it does not rejoice in the wrong but rejoices in the right. No wonder that so many weddings recite this text during the ceremony.

Today, though, I want to go beyond a *description* of love and talk to you about a *depiction*. Instead of talking theoretically about love, let's show that love in action—in real life. Here is the setting in the Gospel of Mark: Jesus and his disciples had left Capernaum, in Galilee, and traveled to Judea beyond the Jordan. News of Jesus's works and teaching had preceded him, so crowds gathered around to listen.

At times it's a tough crowd. For example, the Pharisees are present. Not all of them are villains, but in the Gospel stories they often stand in for overbearing, nitpicky religious legalism. They come to Jesus to test him and trip him up. To make a long story short, Jesus wins.

Then comes the wonderful narrative about people bringing their children to him. The disciples get irritated at this, but Jesus rebukes them. The best way to think about the kingdom of God, he says, is to look upon these innocent ones. He takes the children in his arms and blesses them.

Suddenly, pushing his way through the crowd, a man runs up, kneels down, and asks Jesus what he needs to do to inherit eternal life. Well, everyone there knows this guy. He's the smug, self-assured rich man in town. Nice house, successful business, several cars in the driveway. But he also really does try to be a good person. Attends church every week, donates generously, once served on the leadership council. He gives to the symphony, the art museum, and the local homeless organization.

His question to Jesus, therefore, about how to inherit eternal life seems to most of the people there to be very self-serving. Those within earshot roll their eyes. "Here he goes again," they all mutter. "He just wants Jesus to tell him what a great person he is."

It had taken Jesus only a few seconds to "get" this guy, by the way, but he does not simply tell him to go away. In fact, he gives the man a spot-on answer: You know what this is all about, Jesus says. Don't kill, don't commit adultery, don't bear false witness, honor your father and mother. You learned those things in Sunday school, so just do them. The rich man sees this as an opportunity to boast just a bit: "I've been doing those things all my life, Rabbi." Again, the eyes roll.

But then comes the critical point in this story. What does Jesus do? He doesn't knock him down a few pegs or dismiss him for the egotistical, conceited person that he is. No. As the text reads, "Jesus, looking at him, loved him."

Now what could that possibly mean . . . that Jesus "loved him"? It means that he went beyond the surface folly of the man and understood him deeply—deeper than the man understood himself. Isn't that at least partly what we mean by loving someone, and by being loved? To return briefly to Paul's letter to the Corinthians, when we love someone, we look to what is good and true and right in them, not to what is wrong.

I think Jesus had a small smile on his face when he turned to the man and said, basically, "Oh, you want to be *perfect* do you? Well, that's another matter. Go sell everything you have and then come, follow me." As the text then reads, the man went away sad and grieving. He had a lot of "stuff." Or maybe he went away deeply conflicted, pondering his life and his choices. Yes, let's say that's what he did. And all because of Jesus deeply knowing him. This story is, as I said at the beginning, a depiction of love, a demonstration of the power of love.

There is a gentleness in truly understanding another. That being said, was there a "lesson" Jesus was teaching the rich man? Maybe. But, again, it's gentle. Continue doing what you're doing. Just be a bit more mindful about it, would you? Live an authentic life. Stop being a narcissist. Consider humility as a long-term goal. The point with your life is not to build yourself up. It's to build *other* people up. You're fine. Just chill. Above all, look beyond yourself for your life's meaning.

Our God, help us to love others, and speak kindly to them, with understanding, even when they are boastful or hurtful or silly. And we pray that other people will love us, even in the midst of our foolishness.

Amen.

MARCH

Knowledge

"A Theology of Uncertainty"

S. THOMAS AQVINAS
Israel ex.
7. MAR.

KNOWLEDGE: *"A Theology of Uncertainty"*

LUKE 2: 41–52

Now every year his parents went to Jerusalem for the festival of the Passover. And when he was twelve years old, they went up as usual for the festival. When the festival was ended and they started to return, the boy Jesus stayed behind in Jerusalem, but his parents did not know it. Assuming that he was in the group of travelers, they went a day's journey. Then they started to look for him among their relatives and friends. When they did not find him, they returned to Jerusalem to search for him. After three days they found him in the temple, sitting among the teachers, listening to them and asking them questions. And all who heard him were amazed at his understanding and his answers. When his parents saw him they were astonished; and his mother said to him, "Child, why have you treated us like this? Look, your father and I have been searching for you in great anxiety." He said to them, "Why were you searching for me? Did you not know that I must be in my Father's house?" But they did not understand what he said to them. Then he went down with them and came to Nazareth, and was obedient to them. His mother treasured all these things in her heart. And Jesus increased in wisdom and in years, and in divine and human favor. (NRSV)

Phil 4: 4–7

Rejoice in the Lord always; again I will say, Rejoice. Let your gentleness be known to everyone. The Lord is near. Do not worry about anything, but in everything by prayer and supplication with thanksgiving let your requests be made known to God. And the peace of God, which surpasses all understanding, will guard your hearts and your minds in Christ Jesus. (NRSV)

The last line from these verses in Paul's letter to the Philippians may be familiar to you. It is often used as a final benediction at the end of a church service. May the peace of God guard your hearts and minds. These words are comforting, to be sure, but there's another way to interpret them. They can be seen as a kind of demand being placed on those preaching a sermon or teaching a class. Attend to *both* our hearts and minds. Our souls *and* our brains. Faith *and* reason.

I think you will not be surprised to hear my opinion that this is not a particularly wonderful time in human history to be bringing a questioning and active mind, informed by history and academic training, upon religious claims—and many other claims, as well. Purges are underway to root out those who don't believe what the authorities believe or whose thoughts and words don't align with those in power. Religious intolerance has been unleashed, and a minority of Christians are now trying to rule over the rest of us.

For sure, there have been worse times in human history, in terms of the stifling of inquiry and free expression in matters of faith—indeed, much worse times—but there have also been better times.

So what's going on, anyway? Here's what I think. I think that if there is one word that sums up the problem with religious expression today it is this one: *certainty.*

How very remarkable, isn't it, that so many different cultures and peoples, in the midst of a complex world and such vexing and profound metaphysical issues—issues that, let's face it, do not admit to proof in a laboratory—can be so . . . *certain* . . . that they are right. And that everyone else is wrong. How remarkable that they can all disagree with each other so much, and yet still be so . . . *certain.*

Now, I know: We all crave a bit of certainty in our lives, don't we? I have felt that way, and I bet you have, too. It's a world with so much disagreement and hostility, that we cannot feel certain even just walking down the street that armed and masked guards won't sweep us off the street. In a world of argument, strife, hatred, and warfare, can't we, please, just come here on Sunday mornings and drink in a little certainty?

Well, sort of. I think we can get to something approaching certainty about a few things, but first we have to pass through the wilderness of uncertainty. Or, tell you what: Let me change metaphors on you. Let me say that it is possible to construct an edifice of certainty about some things, but that edifice has to be built upon what we can call "four pillars of uncertainty."

Four pillars of uncertainty. Here they are.

The first pillar of uncertainty is the uncertainty of Scripture. You know what gets me sometimes? How did it happen, exactly, that from a rich Jewish tradition of seething, roiling engagement and dialogue with scripture, we end up in a situation where many Christians (who are, after all, reformed Jews) seem to feel that, as the bumper stickers and lapel pins have it, "God said it. I believe it. That settles it." In some quarters, we're still having arguments about the teaching of Genesis as scientific "fact" in high school biology classrooms. This is a tremendous failure; I don't know how else to say it.

"What would Jesus do?" Sure, look, I'll tell you what Jesus would do with any current version of the Bible in his hands. You can see what he would do in our Gospel reading today. It's a story that places Jesus squarely in the wonderful Jewish tradition of rabbis debating, disagreeing, affirming some things and rejecting others. Jesus wasn't just sitting there passively agreeing with some learned Rabbi, was he? "The Rabbi said it, and that settles it." He was asking questions, probing, probing, probing. And he was providing his own opinions about the answers to those questions. In other words, he was participating in a divine and human dialogue—a dialogue not just about God's word, but a dialogue *from which* God's word for us emerges.

Perhaps some of you have read the Jewish writings called the Talmud. There, this kind of "scripture as dialogue" is preserved even in print. "The Torah has this to say," but on the other hand, "Maimonides had that to say," but "Rabbi Eliezer had this response," and to that "Rabbi Jonah responded thusly."

It's as if you were reading a Bible with comments written in the margins.

And, in fact, that is exactly how you must read the Bible: as if you had in front of you the opinions of as many people as possible as you read—learned scholars and saints and ordinary people like you and me. The alternative is not a happy one: It is to submit to the *tyranny of the text*, and the tyranny of those who would seek to use their interpretation, their reading of scripture, to wield power.

There is great wisdom in our scriptures: soaring and stirring words of wisdom about God, God's creation, and our place within that creation. And there are also terrible words, untrue words, warlike and violent words, and even words placed by people who just didn't get it into the mouth of Jesus for their own selfish ends. And the only way to discern the difference is to subject everything to the fires of human reason and dialogue. An ancient proverb says it well: "True gold does not fear fire." Do not fear honest and faithful questioning, for only in that way will you discover the truths that set you free.

The second pillar of uncertainty is the uncertainty about our privileged position before God as Christians. Be careful about asserting your position as the chosen people of God. Because you know what? God does not have favorites. God does not have chosen people. It is a grave theological error to construct an idea of God that holds that his love and grace surround one person more than another, one culture more than another, one nation more than another, one religion more than another. Now, don't misunderstand me; what I've just said does not mean that just *anything* said about God, any form of religious expression, is equally valid or uplifting. Don't fall for that kind of easy pluralism. Some forms of religious expression are blasphemous and evil, and they can be found in every tradition and on every continent and in every historical period. But no one starts out with a lead in the race for truth. We are running the same race, and the judge is not playing favorites.

A third pillar of uncertainty is very closely related to the second. While the second erroneous certainty really is rooted in sloppy theology, another related one is rooted in sloppy anthropology: an implicit presumption of the superiority of our position relative to other people—the presumption that everything we need to know about God and God's people is contained within our tradition. We might call this the "uncertainty about completeness." For my own part, I find it impossible to rely solely on the western, Christian tradition to form a coherent picture of God, or a coherent understanding about issues like the problem of evil.

When physical disaster strikes—a tsunami, an earthquake, a tornado, or hurricane—people feel anguish that a loving God could let this happen. Was this the judgment of God against these people? Is God dead? Does God not care? Some sects of Christianity get the response to these occurrences dangerously wrong: Disaster, some say, is the result of God's judgment—evidence of divine vengeance and punishment. This is a terrible, even abusive, form of religion. Maybe no religion has this problem figured out, either—Hindus, Buddhists, Muslims, and more—but I know we would be enriched by learning of their teachings. We need the dialogue among religions if we are possibly to make sense of many things going on in God's world today. Interfaith dialogue enriches all of us.

A fourth and final pillar of uncertainty is what I am going to call an uncertainty about judgment. Part of what I mean here is related to this dialogue I just mentioned that we must engage in among our fellow humans from other cultures and traditions. We will not be able to learn from them if we are first judging them. Be careful about playing the religious superiority card because, believe me, it will be played on you—*is* being played on you. Years ago, when I taught a university course on comparative religion, I would occasionally show my students videos from a wonderful BBC series on world religions. In the video on Hinduism, the BBC interviewer is speaking with an ordinary person, a Hindu woman, about her beliefs and her religious life and practice. Under gentle and good-natured, but also persistent questioning, the interviewer finally gets the woman to admit that he—a white, educated, upper-middle-class Christian from England—must have done something *very bad* in a previous life to have been born a white, educated, upper-middle-class Christian from England. So the lesson here is a familiar one: Do not judge, lest you be judged. For with the judgment you make you will be judged, and the measure you give will be the measure you get.

So there you have it: four pillars of uncertainty. And now, Craig, here we are: We've built these four pillars of uncertainty, and you promised you'd talk about the certainty that can be founded on those pillars. So what is it?

But, hey, look, I'm way over time.

No, seriously, the fact is that I *can't tell you exactly*, because the certainties you will experience will arise out of dialogue within the uncertainty. To be sure, your religious tradition—this religious tradition—is a privileged authority. It is your first port of call on your journey and, hopefully, a constant partner during that journey. The only way we can have a meaningful dialogue is if there is some participant in that dialogue with some sort of particular knowledge or experience. Otherwise, dialogue is simply the blind leading the blind.

But you need to look at that authority as something that must continuously prove itself—an authority that is also willing to learn from you and change. That only happens through constant dialogue—from learning, from relationships, from interactions with other cultures and religions, from engagement with people who delight us and the people who make us really mad, but who are part of the noble and ultimately ennobling human conversation.

Like the beautiful sound of music from a violin—music that comes into being only through the friction we place on the strings—certainty arises out of the friction of human interaction and dialogue.

I think there are many people today, constrained by the wrong approach to certainty, who just need to be able to experience the beauty of the world that arises from trusting that God's knowledge becomes known to us through our constant conversations with each other.

When I was a kid, I would sometimes escape from unhappy things happening inside my home by going outside at night and climbing one of the trees in the backyard. Maybe it was a little frightening at times, to be blown back and forth in the wind from up there, but the sky was clear, and the stars were brilliant. And I knew that the roots of that tree went deep into the earth.

Our roots go deep, too, deep into the knowledge and love of God. That, finally, is the certainty I offer you. The certainty that can grow from deep roots.

Maybe it doesn't sound like it's enough. But it is enough. And it will have to do.

Our God, help us to embrace the knowledge that can come from uncertainty. Help our questioning bring us together in our shared quest for truth.

Amen.

APRIL

Courage

"The Black Hole of Good Friday"

S. IVSTINVS
PHILOSOPH.
MART.
13.
Israel ex
April.

COURAGE:
"The Black Hole of Good Friday"

JOHN 13:34–35

A new commandment I give to you, that you love one another; even as I have loved you, that you also love one another. By this all men will know that you are my disciples, if you have love for one another. (NRSV)

ON THE MORNING OF THE 15TH DAY of the Jewish month, Nisan—which translates to about April 3 in the modern calendar—a man already in great pain from torture after his arrest was laid out on his back, and his wrists were nailed to a long horizontal beam of wood. That crossbar was then lifted up onto a vertical post, forming a cross. His feet were then nailed to that upright. His crucifixion was a cruel, agonizing death, something I will discuss in more detail. As I will argue later, Jesus's crucifixion on this day was not just an inconceivable tragedy; its power sucked all the light out of the universe, leaving us with what I call the Great Black Hole of Good Friday.

But how did Jesus get to this point, anyway?

Over the course of his ministry, Jesus's understanding of himself had evolved. He may at first have seen himself as part of a broader prophetic movement within Judaism. In time, his experiences and study of the scriptures had convinced him that he was the Messiah. But there was a catch: He did not understand himself as a conquering hero, as many expected, but rather a sacrificial one. Given that understanding of what "Messiah" means, he believed he had to die. It took supreme courage to finally agree to his fate. He knew what awaited him, but he went to Jerusalem anyway.

So that is what's on Jesus's mind as he arrives in Jerusalem on the day we now celebrate as Palm Sunday. His dramatic entrance on a lowly donkey, with crowds cheering him, made both the Jewish and Roman leaders nervous. Some in the crowd had chanted, "Hosanna to the Son of David," revealing their belief that Jesus was the conquering Messiah who would overturn and defeat the Romans.

There were other Jewish prophets hanging around Jerusalem at about that same period claiming to be a Messiah. Most of them, including John the Baptist, had eventually been killed as a threat to the empire. Was Jesus going to try to create some sort of revolution, threatening the existing order? He was being watched closely.

It did not take Jesus long to press the point about his identity. The first thing he did was to enter the temple and create chaos. He drove out those who were selling and buying in the temple, throwing down the seats of those selling pigeons, and overturning the tables of the money changers. He yelled, "It is written, 'My house shall be called a house of prayer' but you have made it a den of thieves."

He clearly wasn't trying to make friends, was he? It's almost as if he were saying, "Here I am. Come and get me." Indeed, soon thereafter, the chief priests and elders met with the high priest, Caiaphas, to figure out how best to arrest Jesus and have him killed.

On the day we call Thursday, Jesus gathered with his twelve closest disciples to celebrate the Passover meal. Piecing together what might really have happened the awful night when Jesus was arrested is almost impossibly difficult, because the Gospels tell complicated and sometimes contradictory stories about events. By the time the Gospels get written down, many decades after Jesus's death, the Last Supper has already had a lot of theology and doctrine attached to it. You can see that in Mark, Matthew, and Luke, where the last meal is now seen as the institution of the Eucharist.

I like the following, simpler version of events: Jesus has been tipped off that Judas has betrayed him and that Caiaphas's guards will be arresting him in the night. Nevertheless, Jesus is determined to observe the Passover meal. He knows that it truly is his "last supper" before being taken away. But, showing great courage, he nevertheless gathered all of them together to eat, even the disciple who has betrayed him. Imagine sitting there like everything was normal.

This is the moment for great drama, isn't it? Like the words of a coach before a big game? Wouldn't this be the right time for the Great Commission from the Gospel of Matthew: "Now go and make disciples of all nations"?

But no. Instead, it's a heart-rending moment of humility: "When you get together like this, to share bread and wine, will you remember me?" This Jesus, who has proclaimed a new kingdom, a new understanding of our relationship with God, simply asks that his friends remember him. And then, a poignant detail shared by John in the reading for today: What is it that Jesus wants to be remembered for? Miracles? Mighty acts? Again, no. What he wants his legacy to be is that his followers simply love one another. He is saying: "All people will know that you are my disciples if you love one another, as I have loved you; that's where your true power resides." It's a small moment that can take your breath away.

Jesus and his disciples then retired for the night to the Mount of Olives, just outside Jerusalem, to a garden called Gethsemane. But Judas had alerted the authorities to where Jesus would be. (They did not want to arrest him when he was surrounded by crowds, lest it cause a revolt.) Judas had left the Passover meal but returned with the guards and a crowd of people armed with clubs. Judas identifies Jesus, who is then arrested.

According to one scholarly analysis of the historical Jesus, "Caiaphas [the High Priest] had Jesus arrested because of his responsibility to put down troublemakers, especially during festivals [such as Passover]. This corresponds perfectly with all the evidence. Jesus had alarmed some people by his attack on the temple . . . because they feared that he might actually influence God. It is highly probable, however, that Caiaphas was primarily or exclusively concerned with the possibility that Jesus would incite a riot. He sent armed guards to arrest Jesus."[3]

After the arrest, Jesus was led to the Jewish ruling council. An intense exchange ensues about who Jesus was claiming to be. Caiphas asks, "Are you the Messiah, the Son of God?" Here's an odd thing: In Mark, Jesus answers directly: "I am." Matthew and Luke change the response to, "You say that I am."

Mark is probably the accurate one, because Caiaphas then stands and rips his robes, a dramatic act performed only in the presence of deep blasphemy. Jesus is mocked and slapped by the high priest's attendants before he is bound and sent to Pontius Pilate, the Roman ruler of Judea. Pilate, after another interrogation, sends Jesus to Herod, the ruler of Galilee, who promptly sends him back to Pilate for a final decision about whether Jesus should be crucified—something Pilate finally assents to.

I am going to describe, in sometimes vivid and difficult ways, the abuse Jesus suffered and how he died. These are squeamish things, but I can't make my point about the courage of Jesus without these descriptions. We have to know what really happened.

Back with Pilate, Jesus endured great torture. He was beaten by the Roman soldiers, who also put a crown of thorns on his head. Blood would have rolled down his head and into his eyes. The soldiers spat on him and beat him, and he was flogged using a whip with pieces of bone or metal at the ends of the straps. It caused deep lacerations and extreme pain.

The next stop was Golgotha, where the crucifixion was to take place. As I said, the details of his killing are difficult to hear, but we must.

Crucifixion was a terrible death, reserved mostly for hardened criminals and those thought to be threats to Rome. It was not just a punishment; it was also a way to humiliate and publicly shame the condemned.

With long nails pounded through his wrists and feet, and following his previous torture, he was bleeding and in severe agony.

3. Sanders, *The Historical Figure of Jesus*, 269.

Imagine him screaming in pain. As he hung from the cross, the problem then became how to breathe. Sagging down from his arms, his breathing would have been blocked. The only way to breathe was to push up from his damaged feet and pull up from his damaged wrists, long enough to take a breath. This, over and over until, exhausted, he sagged down for the last time and perished from suffocation. The Gospels say he lasted three hours on the cross, but I seriously doubt it. In the state Jesus was in, his death may have come in less than an hour.

So here is my central question: Presuming that the details of death by crucifixion were known throughout the region, what kind of person would voluntarily give himself up to such a death?

Answer: A person of deep courage willing to follow through on his calling and ministry until the bitter end. Jesus knew what was coming, and he did it anyway. We can learn something from this courage. In fact, we can see examples of such courage throughout history in stories like people's resistance to authoritarian regimes, even at risk of their lives. We, too, may be asked to stand up against authoritarianism and fascism. We need courage to speak up against injustice in the world. Against suffering, poverty, famine, and war.

The end of the crucifixion story tells the tale of a deep darkness that fell over the earth for three hours. It is a fitting metaphor for Jesus's death. What Good Friday is, as I said at the beginning, is actually a Great Black Hole, drawing in all the light of the world; drawing in Jesus's life and his teaching; drawing in his followers as well as those that killed him; drawing in all of us—all that we have and all that we hope for. As Jesus breathes his last, we feel as if we have been left utterly alone in a cold and dark universe, suffering and afraid.

But we know something that the Romans didn't. We know that the darkness will not last forever.

Our God, give us courage even in the face of our deepest fears.

Amen.

MAY

Hope

"The Hard Work of Hope"

S.GREGORIVS
NANZIA.
SAPIENTI
9.
Israel ex
MAI,

Hope:
"The Hard Work of Hope"

Matt 6: 28–30

Consider the lilies of the field, how they grow; they neither toil nor spin, yet I tell you, even Solomon in all his glory was not clothed like one of these. But if God so clothes the grass of the field, which is alive today and tomorrow is thrown into the fire, will he not much more clothe you? (NRSV)

Rom 5: 1–5

Therefore, since we have been justified through faith, we have peace with God through our Lord Jesus Christ, through whom we have gained access by faith into this grace in which we now stand. And we boast in the hope of sharing the glory of God. And not only that, but we also glory in our sufferings, because we know that suffering produces perseverance; perseverance produces character; and character produces hope. And hope does not disappoint us, because God's love has been poured out into our hearts through the Holy Spirit, who has been given to us. (NRSV)

Write a sermon on the topic of hope, I said. That should be fairly straightforward, I said. It seems to be a topic we all know something about. Consider Paul, writing in his first letter to the Corinthians, who offers his insight into the three primary theological virtues that are always present amid the chaos of our lives: faith, love, and hope. This is easy, I said. Faith is based on promises made in the past; love is rooted in the demands of the present; and hope looks to the future.

It didn't turn out to be quite that simple.

For example: With what attitude do we look to that future? With what mindset? What are we thinking about when we hope? I fear that too often, hope means something rather simplistic—wishing and desiring, even if circumstances indicate that the wish may not come true. You lose your wallet in an airport boarding area just before getting on the plane. Well, you can always "hope" that someone will return it to you. But it's doubtful. In fact, understood this way, hope feels like kind of a weak emotion. A, "Well, we can always hope" kind of hopeless hope.

But that can't be right, can it? Let's turn to what Jesus said about hope. That's actually more challenging than you might expect, because in his teachings and lessons, Jesus never actually uses the word for "hope."

But the idea of hope is deeply engrained in his teaching, such as the one from the Gospel of Matthew which we just read—one of the most beautiful and meaningful passages in all of scripture. Consider the lilies. If God so clothes the grass of the field, will he not all the more clothe you—that is, take care of all parts of your life?

But Jesus is not actually speaking of vain wishes and desires here. He's talking about something more like "assurance" or even "certainty" that these things will come to pass. It's not hopeless hope, it's confidence. God *will* clothe you.

We see this play out also in Jesus's teachings about the coming of the kingdom of God. In the Gospel of Mark, we hear Jesus at the beginning of his ministry: "The kingdom of God has come near," he says. "Repent and believe the good news!"

In Matthew, he says that the kingdom of God has come upon us. In Luke, not only is the kingdom of God already here, but it resides within us.

Again, this is not some dreamy, hazy kind of wishing. It is *assurance* that the coming of the kingdom of God has already happened or is about to happen. Not vain hope; assurance.

Now we come to a difficult passage from Paul's letter to the Romans, which we just read. I want to do a pretty close reading of these words, so follow along in the bulletin if you can. I can easily make sense of some of what Paul is saying, but other parts are less clear. So let's look: First, we can glory in our sufferings or tribulations, says Paul, because those sufferings produce perseverance. So far, so good. I get that. When we are taxed or tested in any way, mentally, physically, or spiritually, we get stronger; we learn persistence and how to have a stubborn will. And that perseverance, he goes on to say, produces character. Still understandable. Persevering over time produces character or strength or virtue. We learn from those sufferings how to stand firm in who we are.

But now what of the last line? We know that character produces . . . what? Out of nowhere, almost, comes this word "hope." "Character produces hope." This really changes things. Hope is not justified when it comes from mere wishing, Paul seems to be saying. It is justified when it comes from deep within our character and our understanding of the world and our place in it. Hope is a choice we make out of our strength and our ability to live who we are.

I have sensed in recent years an ongoing effort from many quarters to claim an energetic, actionable sense of hope from the clutches of vain wishing. These efforts promote the idea that hope is not only the envisioning of the future, *but also* the hard work of helping to make that future a reality.

Consider this dramatic insight drawn from a social media posting. (It is difficult to credit because it is from an anonymous Twitter account.[4]) It reads, "People speak of hope as if it is this delicate, ephemeral thing made of whispers and spider's webs. It's not. Hope has dirt on her face, blood on her knuckles, the grit of the cobblestones in her hair, and just spat out a tooth as she rises for another go."

Does this hit home as a believable, authentic idea of what hope is? I suspect you are struggling, as I did. But I'm starting to get it.

4. Matthew (@CrowsFault), March 10, 2022.

Let me then add some insights from bell hooks, the late cultural critic and author. According to her writings, hope is a strong reaction to the injustices of the world. Hope is essential in the fight for social justice and the liberation of marginalized people. She saw hope not just as wishful thinking or passive optimism, but as an active force that fuels resistance and activism.[5]

Hope, in this context, is rooted in the belief that change is possible, even in the face of oppression or difficult circumstances. It requires not just idealism but action, solidarity, struggle, and an ongoing commitment to challenging systems of power.

So what are we left with here? What are some conclusions we can come to at the close of our exploration into hope? Consider some of the words that have arisen during this discussion: action, change, struggle, liberation, solidarity, character, perseverance. Not passive or weak words, are they?

I have no choice but to declare hope to have a far more active and even proactive mindset about both present and future than we might have previously presumed. It is not about *wishing* but *doing*. Not just idealism but also *action*.

This is a difficult and challenging teaching, and I think we need to spend some time prayerfully considering what practical implications this insight has to our lives, especially in the near term.

"Hope begins in the dark," author Anne Lamott has written, "the stubborn hope that if you just show up and try to do the right thing, the dawn will come. You wait and watch and work: you don't give up."[6]

Our God, help us to show up and try. Help us have the courage to hope and then to bring about what we hope for.

Amen

5. Hooks, *Teaching Community*, 122.

6. Lamott, Anne, X, March 18, 2022. https://x.com/ANNELAMOTT/status/1472606700288942085.

JUNE

JUSTICE

"Tough-Minded and Tender-Hearted"

S·SILVERIVS
PAP·ET.
M.
20.
Isrüel ex.
Iuni

Justice:
"Tough-Minded and Tender-Hearted"

Matt 10: 16–20

See, I am sending you out like sheep into the midst of wolves; so be wise as serpents and innocent as doves. Beware of them, for they will hand you over to councils and flog you in their synagogues; and you will be dragged before governors and kings because of me, as a testimony to them and the Gentiles. When they hand you over, do not worry about how you are to speak or what you are to say; for what you are to say will be given to you at that time; for it is not you who speak, but the Spirit of your Father speaking through you. (NRSV)

Matt 23:23

Woe to you, teachers of the law and Pharisees, you hypocrites! You give a tenth of your spices—mint, dill and cumin. But you have neglected the more important matters of the law—justice, mercy and faithfulness. You should have practiced the latter, without neglecting the former. (NRSV)

I WANT US TO IMAGINE A SITUATION where our society and nation, and we as individuals—you and me—are at peace. (It's a fantasy, but go with me here.) All parts of society or of our souls are in harmony; people are integrated with each other and within themselves and, consequently, more capable of living a fulfilling life. People can reason well, keep desires in check, and act in accordance with virtue. Individuals are treated with fairness and equality and their rights are protected.

This is a state called "justice." According to the Greek philosophers Plato and Aristotle, the ultimate purpose of justice is to actually achieve the well-being, the flourishing, the excellence of individuals and society as a whole. Let me repeat part of that: Justice helps us flourish; it enables us to achieve excellence. It is not oppressive; it is not socialism or communism. Nations exist to promote a just life. Justice is a key part of creating a stable and harmonious society. The laws of nations must align with the principles of justice to ensure the good life for their citizens. To speak more plainly, a commitment to justice is what holds everything together.

Let me try to bring those abstract principles to life a bit.

One way is for us to look at sermons from Dr. Martin Luther King, Jr.—obviously a good choice for insights about justice. In one sermon, King quotes the passage from Matthew we just read: I am sending you out as sheep into the midst of wolves; so be wise as serpents and innocent as doves. "The good life," King writes, "combines the toughness of the serpent and the tenderness of the dove." To only be a serpent means you may become passionless and hard-hearted. "The hard-hearted individual," says King, "never sees people as people, but rather as mere objects or as impersonal cogs in an ever-turning wheel." [7]

Hard-heartedness was what characterized the so-called "robber barons" of the late nineteenth century—people like Rockefeller, Vanderbilt, Carnegie, and J.P Morgan. They amassed vast fortunes through unscrupulous, exploitative, and often monopolistic practices. They used their wealth and power to manipulate markets, suppress workers, and undermine competition for personal gain. These kinds of robber barons are coming back into prominence again as the twenty-first century progresses.

7. King, *Strength to Love*, 78.

We also see hard-heartedness in the actions and words of Yahweh, the God of the Hebrew Bible. Too often, God's understanding of justice looks like pure vengeance. Vengeance is mine, and payback, God says in the Book of Deuteronomy. He saw unfaithfulness among his people "and was jealous." "He said, 'I will hide my face from them; . . . For the day of [my people's] calamity is at hand.'"

"For a fire is kindled by my anger," this God also says, "and burns to the depths of Sheol; it devours the earth and its increase and sets on fire the foundations of the mountains. I will heap disasters upon them, spend my arrows against them—a wasting hunger, burning consumption, bitter pestilence. The teeth of beasts I will send against them, with venom of things crawling in the dust." Nasty stuff.

We also see terrible statements of vengeful thinking in many of the Psalms, such as Psalm 137, where the psalmist calls on the Lord to bring vengeance on those who destroyed Jerusalem. "Blessed is the one," the Psalm reads, "who seizes your children and smashes them against the rock."

I don't see theological wisdom here; I see a vengeful supernatural being. I'm inclined to look elsewhere for truth about justice.

So we see the negative repercussions from being too hard-hearted. But there is another error in the search for justice, according to King. To be *only* dovelike risks becoming too accepting of the status quo—too soft-minded, acquiescent, sentimental, and anemic.

There is a need, says King, for a tough mind—not a hard-hearted one. "The tough mind is sharp and penetrating," King writes. It is characterized by "incisive thinking, realistic appraisal, and decisive judgment." It is necessary to counter humankind's gullibility—their tendency to stick with "easy answers and half-baked solutions."

Few people, he says, "have the toughness of mind to judge critically and to discern the true from the false, the fact from the fiction. . . . One of the great needs of [humankind] is to be lifted above the morass of false propaganda." False fears "leave the soft-minded haggard by day and haunted by night." [8]

Jesus knew what this balance between tough-mindedness and soft-heartedness was all about. Consider the second Gospel reading for the day, from Matthew. The Pharisees and their compatriots had, according to Jesus, a small-minded, hard-hearted view of justice—being persnickety in small matters like the tithing of spices, but then not honoring more relevant things that address the actual needs of human beings in this moment.

"You have neglected the more important matters of the law—justice, mercy, and faithfulness," Jesus says. "You should have practiced the latter, without neglecting the former." If you wish for absolute allegiance to the rule of law, then you must also have absolute allegiance to justice and mercy.

I will leave you with an important insight: We spend a lot of time speaking of justice in terms of the functioning of a nation, extending especially to the area of social justice. This is good and proper. Justice refers in part to the broader social and economic structures of our nation and of all nations, ensuring that society upholds the dignity and rights of every individual, especially the vulnerable.

But never forget that the concept of justice applies to our personal lives as well as to societies and nations. You might take the time, even later today, to look at your own life to determine what balance you have achieved between both tough-mindedness and tender-heartedness.

I deeply suspect that the people who are the most successful in promoting justice in our nation and in the world are those who have also achieved justice within themselves.

Our God, help us to achieve justice in our lives and in the world. Amen.

8. King, *Strength to Love*, 95.

JULY

LIBERTY

"St. Paul's Declaration of Independence"

S. ELIAS
PROPHET
20.
Julij
Israel ex.

Liberty:
"St. Paul's Declaration of Independence"

American Declaration of Independence

We hold these truths to be self-evident, that all men are created equal, that they are endowed by their Creator with certain unalienable Rights, that among these are Life, Liberty and the pursuit of Happiness. —That to secure these rights, Governments are instituted among Men, deriving their just powers from the consent of the governed, —That whenever any Form of Government becomes destructive of these ends, it is the Right of the People to alter or to abolish it, and to institute new Government, laying its foundation on such principles and organizing its powers in such form, as to them shall seem most likely to effect their Safety and Happiness.[9]

2 Cor 3: 7–8; 12–18

Now if the ministry of death, chiseled in letters on stone tablets, came in glory so that the people of Israel could not gaze at Moses's face because of the glory of his face, a glory now set aside, how much more will the ministry of the Spirit come in glory? . . . Since, then, we have such a hope, we act with complete frankness, not like Moses, who put a veil over his face to keep the people of Israel from gazing at the end of the glory that was being set aside. But

9. "Declaration of Independence: A Transcription," National Archives, https://www.archives.gov/founding-docs/declaration-transcript

their minds were hardened. Indeed, to this very day, when they hear the reading of the old covenant, the same veil is still there; it is not unveiled since in Christ it is set aside. Indeed, to this very day whenever Moses is read, a veil lies over their minds, but when one turns to the Lord, the veil is removed. Now the Lord is the Spirit, and where the Spirit of the Lord is, there is freedom. And all of us, with unveiled faces, seeing the glory of the Lord as though reflected in a mirror, are being transformed into the same image from one degree of glory to another, for this comes from the Lord, the Spirit. (NRSV)

So here we are, in *July*. This is the month in America when thoughts turn to the founding years of the country. At least, sort of. Children recite great speeches. Bands play patriotic music. Towns hold parades. Families host picnics.

What is at the heart of this holiday? Well, honestly, I think it's blowing things up. Not kidding, actually. But second in line, what is it?

I think it's safe to say that the common theme is freedom—liberty. July 4th, after all, marks a founding event—the date when one of our essential documents, the Declaration of Independence, was released in 1776. With it, we declared liberty from the rule of an oppressive monarch, out of touch with the people and out of line with seventeenth- and eighteenth-century philosophies about government, freedom, and self-determination.

Several decades ago, my wife and I were able to share some day-hiking in Norway with a retired couple from the US. He had actually been a geologist, helping to map and manage huge swaths of land across the American West. But his passion was history. I no longer remember how we got on the topic of the country's founders, but he made one thing quite clear: It was nearly a miracle that things came together as they did for the infant country.

We were lucky that there were people at the helm for whom reason and logic were triumphing over sectarian religious thinking. Key movers and shakers began to acknowledge that this country of ours was declaring itself free from religious oppression and rule, as well as rule by kings.

But it wasn't ordained that it should go that way. Slave owners and loyalists were opposed to independence from British rule, joined by other groups such as some Catholics, African Americans, and German and Dutch settlers.

Somehow, reason and a new order prevailed. Oppressive law was thrown off and eventually, after hard years of war, liberty from an oppressive government prevailed.

One thing to bear in mind, as my new friend on a Norwegian trail insisted, is that what the founders proposed was radical. All humans are created equal; everyone has the right to the pursuit of happiness, to life, to liberty. Government is only legitimate if it is derived from the consent of the governed. We take these statements for granted now but, back then, this was new thinking—the beginning of what we refer to as the American "experiment."

Is that the most radical expression of liberty ever written? Actually, I have another candidate. As my vote for words that are truly radical in their claims for freedom, let me propose Paul's second letter to the Corinthians, of which we read a long passage this morning. Please follow along with me, if you'd like, as I walk us through some key parts of the text.

But first, context. The broader subject here is what obligations followers of Jesus have to Mosaic law as found in the first five books of the Hebrew Bible—the Torah, part of the set of books that Christians usually call the "Old Testament." Understanding these obligations was a problem from the earliest years of the infant church. One big issue had to do with whether non-Jewish converts, such as the Gentiles, nevertheless had to be circumcised. The law going back to Genesis was clear: Every male should be circumcised as a sign of the covenant between God and his people. This is reaffirmed in the Mosaic law (particularly in Leviticus and Exodus).

You might well imagine this was an obstacle to converting non-Jews.

Paul became quite vehement about this topic. No, he said, in his first letter to the Corinthians, chapter seven: If you were uncircumcised when you were called to Christ, then circumcision is not needed. Elsewhere, in Galatians, he angrily writes that traditional Jews who remain insistent and vexatious about circumcision should "cut theirs off."

Paul's vehemence about the Mosaic law continues in his second letter to the church at Corinth.

Right off the bat in chapter three, Paul goes on the offensive. He contrasts the Law with the spirit of the living God. Faith is focused on the human heart, not on stone tablets—meaning, of course, the tablets Moses received from God on Mt. Sinai.

He goes on to say that God has made him qualified to be a "minister of a new covenant." Again, not the letter of law but of Spirit. "The letter kills," Paul writes, "but the Spirit gives life." Then he goes on to equate the letters on stone tablets with what he calls, "the ministry of death." Elsewhere he calls it the "ministry of condemnation." Strong stuff, isn't it?

Paul also refers to the time, in Exodus, when Moses descended from Mt. Sinai with the two stone tablets of the Law. His face was radiant because he had spoken with God. So radiant, in fact, that the Israelites were afraid to approach him, so Moses wore a veil over his face to cover the brightness.

Paul uses this "veil" as a metaphor for not recognizing the Spirit of God. He writes, "To this very day, when they [meaning, adherents of the old Law] hear the reading of the old covenant, the same veil is still there." In Christ, however, it is set aside. "Indeed, to this very day whenever Moses is read," Paul writes, "a veil lies over their minds, but when one turns to the Lord, the veil is removed."

Listen to Paul's conclusion to this declaration of independence from the Law: "Now the Lord is the Spirit, and where the Spirit of the Lord is, there is freedom. And all of us, with unveiled faces, seeing the glory of the Lord as though reflected in a mirror, are being transformed into the same image from one degree of glory to another, for this comes from the Lord, the Spirit."

Christians have endured and perpetuated two millennia of confusion when it comes to interpretation of the Mosaic Law and other commandments and directions from the Hebrew Bible, often ignoring what Paul has to say about the law here in Second Corinthians. I will be brutally honest with you. I think some people quote the Law and other books of scripture when it serves their purposes and ignore them when they do not.

For example, we often quote lovely passages from the Psalms, like Psalm 96: "Let the heavens rejoice, let the earth be glad; let the sea resound, and all that is in it."

But then we ignore other psalms that are less, shall we say, pleasurable or edifying or even family friendly. Consider Psalm 139, in which the psalmist asks God to slay the wicked. Or Psalm 58, where God is asked to break the teeth of enemies, treating them as a garden slug or a stillborn child. Rough stuff.

You see? Use of the Hebrew Bible and the Mosaic Law in particular is often cherry-picking, with sometimes unfortunate consequences. We have far-right evangelicals and Christian nationalists who quote Leviticus because they do not accept gay people; and Genesis because they do not tolerate trans people. They trot out vicious language about homosexuals, but they proceed to ignore other instances when the death sentence is to be applied to people like adulterers, those who curse or strike their parents, those who do not go to church, and more. Cherry-picking. Do you know someone, private or public, who has cheated on their spouse or failed to attend church? Should they be stoned for their behavior? The question may make you uncomfortable, but the clear answer from Mosaic Law is yes.

So what do we do? Clearly, those who have committed adultery or ignored the Sabbath are not going to be stoned. In fact, no one is going to be stoned (in most of the free world) for their moral or religious behavior, and that's a good thing. But what are we going to do with the Mosaic Law?

I think we do what reasonable, educated people do in the twenty-first century. I think we look for reason-directed thinking wherever we can find it. I'm not cherry picking; I'm just not presuming that Biblical texts are always to be considered as authoritative. They need to prove their authority to us, as educated people. This guideline applies to the Christian scriptures as well—verses about women not speaking in the church, or verses justifying slavery. The need to prove the authority of the Bible means there might be some cherries, or no cherries, or a lot of cherries in scripture. But it's up to us to decide. Our freedom from Biblical tyranny depends on it.

But now comes a key question to be asked: Now that we know we are released by the Spirit of God from the false authority and bondage of the Mosaic Law, what then are we supposed to do? It sounds daunting, doesn't it?

In fact, though, we are not just thrown into the deep end of the pool here. We have a *lot* of resources at hand. Thanks to those, we are smarter than the biblical texts. Always. It's an important point. We know more than most Bible writers did 2,000 to 3,000 years ago. You may not believe that but it's true. We know more about science, for example, and government. Human rights. Equality. Freedom. The pursuit of happiness.

We have millennia of insights from philosophers, scientists, theologians, social scientists, psychologists. With critical analysis and interpretation, we might even look at the Mosaic Law and find scraps of wisdom we can apply to our lives. (Here's a hint: The strictures that we should not kill or lie or steal seem like keepers.) Unconstrained by old doctrine and beliefs, we can accept what we regard as wise within the Bible and reject what seems foolish.

Living outside of the most stringent parts of Mosaic Law may seem an awesome challenge to you, but I assure you that your education has more than prepared you to look critically at Biblical texts and subject them to hard questioning. This is important because, without that approach, you are at the mercy of those who would interpret texts to fulfill their small-minded, sectarian, sometimes abusive goals.

As the authors of the American Declaration of Independence wrote, "when a long train of abuses and usurpations . . . [reveals] a design to reduce [people] under absolute Despotism, it is their right, it is their duty, to throw off such Government, and to provide new Guards for their future security." Those are tough words, but we have to take them and evaluate them as written.

Likewise, it is not only our right but our duty to throw off the "ministry of death and condemnation" inherent in parts of books like Exodus, Leviticus, and Deuteronomy. Again, Paul is using tough words, but we have to take them as he wrote them.

It is our duty to throw off the shackles of the law, and accept the glory of the Spirit, who came not to condemn but to save. There is freedom and acceptance and glory in that outcome. May we have just a taste of that salvation and that liberty. Then we'll want more.

Our God, help us learn to be free.

Amen.

AUGUST

JUDGMENT

"If That's How You Want to Play the Game"

S.MARIA AD NIVES
Israel ex.
5. AVG.

Judgment:
"If That's How You Want to Play the Game"

John 8: 1–11

Early in the morning he came again to the temple. All the people came to him and he sat down and began to teach them. The scribes and the Pharisees brought a woman who had been caught in adultery; and making her stand before all of them, they said to him, "Teacher, this woman was caught in the very act of committing adultery. Now in the law Moses commanded us to stone such women. Now what do you say?" They said this to test him, so that they might have some charge to bring against him. Jesus bent down and wrote with his finger on the ground. When they kept on questioning him, he straightened up and said to them, "Let anyone among you who is without sin be the first to throw a stone at her." And once again he bent down and wrote on the ground. When they heard it, they went away, one by one, beginning with the elders; and Jesus was left alone with the woman standing before him. Jesus straightened up and said to her, "Woman, where are they? Has no one condemned you?" She said, "No one, sir." And Jesus said, "Neither do I condemn you. Go your way, and from now on do not sin again." (NRSV)

Matt 5:27–32

You have heard that it was said, "You shall not commit adultery." But I say to you that everyone who looks at a woman with lust has already committed adultery with her in his heart. If your right eye causes you to sin, tear it out and throw it away; it is better for you to lose one of your members than for your whole body to be thrown into hell. And if your right hand causes you to sin, cut it off and throw it away; it is better for you to lose one of your members than for your whole body to go into hell. It was also said, "Whoever divorces his wife, let him give her a certificate of divorce." But I say to you that anyone who divorces his wife, except on the ground of sexual immorality, causes her to commit adultery, and whoever marries a divorced woman commits adultery. (NRSV)

I *want to begin* with a couple of "just supposes" or "what-ifs." Suppose you are reading a book that is really a collection of lecture notes taken by students of a very famous professor. But suppose that the book you have keeps puzzling you . . . in some chapters the professor seems to be saying one thing; in the next chapter, he appears to be saying something almost exactly opposite.

In cases like that, I think you've really got three options in trying to figure it all out. Option 1 is that the professor was confused or immature, developing his thinking and not yet consistent. Option 2 is that the person was devious . . . saying one thing to one group and another thing to another group. (This happens in politics sometimes, doesn't it, when a politician says what a crowd wants to hear.)

Option 3 is that the people recording the event for posterity just plain got it wrong. Students might remember different things, or misinterpret notes, or—if the professor was famous—add what they *wished* he had said to help their movement along. Sometimes they might come close to his intent; other times, they put words in his mouth that would have him spinning in his grave.

OK . . . a long preamble, I know . . . but I need this background to help us understand how we can reconcile those times when we're reading the Gospels and Jesus seems to be saying things that really contradict things he says elsewhere.

That's the reason, in part, that I've paired the two Gospel readings this morning. Here we have this wonderful story from the Gospel of John . . . an exemplary story of what Jesus and his ministry were really all about. The local big shots bring this woman to Jesus. "Hey, Jesus," they say. "Here's a sinful woman. We caught her in the act. Our Law says she is to be stoned for it. What do you say?" Well, what is Jesus to say? The local big shots are right, of course. The Law in Deuteronomy demanded execution for adultery.

Jesus's response is something like the following: "Yes, you're right. I know what the Law says. Well, if that's the way you want to play the game, then here's what I suggest. The people who are to do this stoning, then, must themselves be pure and sinless, don't you all agree? If you're going to interpret the Law this way, then let's be consistent."

The reason I call this story exemplary is that one of the primary characteristics of Jesus's ministry was his welcoming into the kingdom of God all those most despised by the rest of his society—sinners, harlots, lepers, tax collectors. Now, this isn't just some weak, "anything goes" kind of welcome; remember, the story does end, "Go and sin no more." But the point is that Jesus opened his arms—opened God's arms, really—and welcomed into the kingdom everyone. *Everyone.* No exceptions.

But now we come to the harder part. If, like me, you believe that this radical welcome of sinners into the kingdom of God defines Jesus's ministry, then what are you to do with those passages of the Bible that are much grimmer, much more judgmental? In our other reading today, from Matthew, not only does Jesus appear to be embracing those words of Deuteronomy, he's making them even stricter. Not just being caught in the act, he says. Even if you've looked at someone and had what we might call "dirty thoughts," that makes you an adulterer, too. And if your eye causes you to sin, better pluck it out. If your hand causes you to sin, better cut it off.

Well, there it is. What are we to do?

Remember the three options I gave you earlier. Option 1 is that the person was confused or immature. Option 2 is that the person is devious. If you don't mind, I'm going to reject those options here this morning.

Which leaves us option 3: Jesus's interpreters got it wrong somehow. (By the way, notice that I do not give you another option—call it option 4—because it grieves me, frankly, to see this one foisted upon too many contemporary Christians: *"If I can't make sense of this, it must be my fault."* No, I reject that one utterly. God gave us a mind, so use it.)

So if Jesus's interpreters got it wrong, in what way might they have gotten it wrong, and why? Remember that the Bible you are reading has been through several languages in translation. Jesus was speaking in Aramaic. The earliest manuscripts we have are in Greek, and then we have those translated into English. Certain nuances of language are inevitably going to be lost. For example, novelist Kurt Vonnegut once suggested that Jesus's words, "the poor are always with you," were actually a bit of humor: "Don't worry, there'll still be plenty of poor people left after I'm gone."

With this bit of background, let's revisit these hard words of Matthew. I think there really is some historical bit of truth to them. But here was the context. Let's bring in our sinful woman again from the Gospel of John. "Jesus," the scribes and Pharisees say, "Here's this sinner. The law says we are to cut off this evil from Israel. What do you say?"

And Jesus replies, "Really? Is that the way you want to play this game? You want to cut her off completely? Well, then, if your eye causes you to sin, why don't you pluck it out? If your hand causes you to sin, why don't you cut it off? Isn't it better to go into the kingdom without a hand or an eye than to be damned for all time?" Jesus' response is to say, in effect, it makes no more sense to cut this sinner off from the body of God's people than it makes sense to cut off your hand or poke out your eye.

Jesus presses the point: "And you who condemn adultery—haven't you looked with desire yourself? Haven't you made loopholes in the Law for divorce? If you apply the standard so strictly, you too stand condemned."

The Gospel of John tells the ending of this confrontation very dramatically. One by one, the people assembled consider what Jesus has said, and they simply leave. At the end, the woman is alone with Jesus. "Woman," he says, "So where are they all? Is there no one left to condemn you?" "No sir," she says. "Not a single person." "I don't condemn you either," Jesus says. "And God doesn't condemn you. Now go and renew your life." Sort of like the wise judge looking down at a boy who's been caught stealing but is basically an OK kid. "Get out of here now," says the judge. "And don't let me see you before this court again."

I doubt whether, in reality, these confrontations Jesus had with the ruling religious authorities ever ended quite so dramatically and cleanly. It's hard to imagine them just giving up and walking away. Their real talent, after all, was in arguing fine points of the law.

But the power of that ending is really in its portrayal of a human being left alone, finally, with Jesus, who does not condemn her. I suggest to you that this gives us something to go away with here today. For those of us who are adults, it would be difficult for any of us to have lived this long without at least a few things weighing on our souls. We know our own sins, and even if we have not been condemned for them in some way, we still carry the condemnation of the world in our hearts, secretly, every day.

So I invite you to imagine: You are brought by your accusers to Jesus. He listens, then quietly sends them all away. And there you are, alone with him. You can hardly meet his gaze. But then you hear his voice: "They cannot condemn you. I do not condemn you. And, most important, God does not condemn you."

Filled with the glory of God's grace and love, you turn, stunned, to walk away. Then Jesus calls your name one last time. He has a bit of a smile on his face. "And don't let me see you before this court again."

Our God, help us to forgive others, and to forgive ourselves.

Amen.

SEPTEMBER

Joy

"Training to Be Joyful"

S. BERTINVS ABBAS.
Israël ex.
5. Sept.

Joy:
"Training to Be Joyful"

John 15: 10–11

If you keep my commandments, you will abide in my love, just as I have kept my Father's commandments and abide in his love. I have said these things to you so that my joy may be in you and that your joy may be complete. (NRSV)

Gal 5: 16–18; 22–25

So I say, walk by the Spirit, and you will not gratify the desires of the flesh. For the flesh desires what is contrary to the Spirit, and the Spirit what is contrary to the flesh. They are in conflict with each other, so that you are not to do whatever you want. But if you are led by the Spirit, you are not under the law. . . . The fruit of the Spirit is love, joy, peace, forbearance, kindness, goodness, faithfulness, gentleness, and self-control. Against such things there is no law. Those who belong to Christ Jesus have crucified the flesh with its passions and desires. Since we live by the Spirit, let us keep in step with the Spirit. (NRSV)

It is a joy to preach this sermon on the topic of, yes, "joy." Why does it give me joy? And what is joy, anyway—exactly?

One reason I have looked forward to this sermon is that we spent most of the year on some pretty heavy topics—knowledge, courage, justice, judgment. Sometimes we would smile at a particular insight, but just as often we might have listened with a grimace and a furrowed brow. Not this topic. There is no way to talk about "joy" without lifting our heads, opening our eyes, taking deep breaths. Feeling something almost primal, but something transcendent as well.

Take a moment to try to capture a memory of joy in your life and tell me where you feel it in your body. For me, it begins in the heart area and goes up through my neck to my head and eyes and tear ducts. An unutterably lovely piece of music or even passage of music can make my eyes water. A simple act of kindness. Beautiful words of hope or peace or solace. I'm guessing you are the same.

In his memoir, *Surprised by Joy*, C.S. Lewis strikes a similar note. Lewis describes joy as an intense, often overwhelming sense of longing, beauty, and desire. This "joy" wasn't happiness in the conventional sense. I think we can all agree that feeling "happy" pales in comparison to feeling "joy."

Joy is something more spontaneous—something comes upon us suddenly, especially when we encounter art, nature, or moments of profound imagination. Lewis refers to this sensation as a "glimpse" of something greater—a glimpse—something beyond the material world. This speaks to an unfortunate aspect of emotional joy. It often does not last very long but is, as Lewis writes, a "glimpse." The gray world cracks open, if only for a moment, letting an eternal light shine through.

Lewis acknowledges that, for much of his life, he did not fully understand what this "joy" was. He describes it as a kind of spiritual hunger or desire for something transcendent—something beyond our ordinary existence. He initially searched for this "joy" in various ways—through literature, philosophy, and other intellectual pursuits—but was unable to find a satisfying answer to what it meant. It was only later, through his religious yearning, that Lewis came to understand this longing as a reflection of the soul's desire for God. [10]

10. Lewis, *Surprised by Joy*, 86.

Doesn't the feeling of joy make you feel that you are in touch with something beyond yourself, beyond our own small lives? As Paul writes in his letter to the Galatians, joy is a fruit of the Spirit: love and joy, along with peace, forbearance, kindness, goodness, faithfulness, gentleness, self-control.

As he then says, since we live by the Spirit, let us keep in step with the Spirit. Joy is not only a fruit of the Spirit, it is a gift of the Spirit, and we should acknowledge it as such.

Now I'm going to spend a few minutes thinking about joy in a slightly different sense. What if joy is not a simple accident—random converging things that surprise us and offer us a glimpse—but more importantly a capacity or capability that we can build that makes it more likely that we will experience that emotion?

You see where I'm going here. What if one can train oneself, or develop the inner capability, to experience joy and actually use it in some essential way. Consider an analogy to wanting to hike in Yosemite National Park. You will enjoy the experience far more if you take the time to train for it. Hiking will seem more spontaneously pleasurable. You will have physical endurance that feels natural.

Some people speak of a concept called, a "glimmer." Glimmers are those moments in a day that make you feel joy, happiness, peace, or gratitude. Once you train your brain to be on the lookout for glimmers, runs this insight, these tiny moments will appear more and more.

We see this insight into the emotions in general, and joy in particular, in the writings of contemporary philosopher Martha Nussbaum. She distinguishes between the achievements we have made in life—like being educated or well-nourished or funny—and the capabilities we use to achieve those conditions. She emphasizes human flourishing as the ultimate goal of social and political arrangements.[11]

She even names some of these capabilities—things like being able to live a normal lifespan; being able to have good health; being able to use the senses and to think, imagine, and reason. An

11. Nussbaum, *Creating Capabilities*, 67.

additional capability focuses in particular on the emotions: being able to form emotional attachments and to express emotions.

Whose responsibility is it to develop this capability to experience an emotion like joy? One answer is simply ourselves. Like hiking in Yosemite, we can't be hapless victims within our own lives. We need to work. We need to train.

In addition, though, society, parents, educational institutions, culture, and government should help ensure that all individuals have the opportunities to develop their capabilities and lead lives of value—lives that can experience emotions like joy. This is not a matter of "wokeness," to use the ugly and insulting word circulating in the early twenty-first century in America. It is a matter of the natural functioning of a virtuous republic.

Nussbaum also reflects on how joy and suffering interact in the context of a real, actual human life. She is particularly interested in how emotions like joy relate to the complexities of vulnerability and the fragility of human existence. Because, let's face it: We are vulnerable; we are fragile. Joy, for her, is deeply tied to our capacity for flourishing, but it is also intertwined with the uncertainty and unpredictability of life.

Let me repeat some of that. How does an overwhelming experience such as joy relate to human fragility and vulnerability? Joy is part of the flourishing of human beings, but also occurs within the uncertainties of life. Maybe we can think of joy as one of those large maps that keep track of our travels. We visit somewhere, and we put a pin in the map to remember it.

I think we can train ourselves to experience joy more regularly in our lives, putting pins into our experiences so we do not forget and so we can experience them in other places and at other times. Perhaps this will also help us bring joy to others.

I was struck by some of the words delivered by President Joe Biden in his eulogy for former President Jimmy Carter, on January 9, 2025. Biden talked about the responsibility not just to feel joy ourselves, but to share it with others as part of our commitment to life itself:

"At our best," Biden said, "we share the better parts of ourselves: joy, solidarity, love, commitment. Not for reward, but in reverence for the incredible gift of life we've all been granted. To make every minute of our time here on Earth count."[12]

Our God, help us train ourselves to live a joyful life.

Amen.

12. "President Joseph Biden's Eulogy from the State Funeral for Former President Jimmy Carter," U.S. Embassy & Consulates in Italy, January 9, 2025.

OCTOBER

Repentance

"The Limits of Forgiveness"

S.SAN
TERESIA
5:
Octob
Israel ex.

Repentance: *"The Limits of Forgiveness"*

Matt 18: 15–17; 21–22

If your brother or sister sins against you, go and point out the fault when the two of you are alone. If you are listened to, you have regained that one. But if you are not listened to, take one or two others along with you, so that every word may be confirmed by the evidence of two or three witnesses. If that person refuses to listen to them, tell it to the church, and if the offender refuses to listen even to the church, let such a one be to you as a gentile and a tax collector. . . .

Then Peter came and said to him, "Lord, if my brother or sister sins against me, how often should I forgive? As many as seven times?" Jesus said to him, "Not seven times, but, I tell you, seventy times seven times." (NRSV)

In the Gospel reading today, we have two different pictures of Christian forgiveness. The first was not spoken by Jesus, but is part of something that might have been a kind of "handbook" of behavior for the early church. (The passage even refers to "the church," meaning Jesus could not have uttered those words because there was no "church" yet.) It sets forth a procedure for dealing with those who have sinned against us, but refuse the necessary steps of repentance and forgiveness. Try to handle the matter in private. Then bring a couple of other people as witnesses.

Then basically expel them. (That's another reason why these words could not have been said by Jesus, who, as you probably recall, sat at table with outcasts like tax collectors and did not condemn them.)

The other passage is something that Jesus probably actually said: We have an obligation to forgive a limitless number of times.

Based on these two passages, I have two sermons to preach today about forgiveness. But don't worry. The first is very short.

I would characterize these sermons in terms of two faces. Think of the first face as beaming, looking upward in wonder and awe. The second face is grimmer: brow furrowed, eyes squinting, a slight frown. Both have to do with the multiple dimensions of forgiveness—our hope to forgive and our hope to be forgiven.

So first sermon, first face: *The wonder of forgiveness.* Forgiveness is one of the best things that our Christian faith has going for it, wouldn't you agree? The transgressor reaching out for renewal and reconciliation, the wounded opening their hearts, embracing the guilty one and wiping the slate clean. What could be more central to our faith?

Poet and philosopher David Whyte has written that to forgive is to assume a larger identity than you were when you were first hurt.[13] Philosopher Hannah Arendt once wrote of forgiveness as an action of freedom, no longer enslaved by the hurtful act—"freeing from its consequences both the one who forgives and the one who is forgiven."[14]

And that's it. That's the sermon. This is a good ending for many. We shake hands as you exit, you smile and praise me for the inspiring words, and we all return to our Sunday afternoons thinking about how we might become more forgiving ourselves.

But now let's consider the second face, a second sermon—grimmer, as I said. It is grim in part because its focus is on the hard work of repentance and penitence that actually sit behind forgiveness.

13. Whyte, *Consolations*, 27.

14. Arendt, *Human Condition*, 42.

This is the time of year that often includes the Jewish holiday, Yom Kippur. The 10-day period between Rosh Hashanah, the Jewish new year, to Yom Kippur, the Day of Atonement, is called "The Ten Days of Repentance." The period is a kind of trial, and an unusual one at that. As one Rabbi has written, most trials are intended to determine responsibility for past deeds. But the verdict of this trial is determined not just by our attitude toward our misdeeds but also by "our attempts to *rectify them by changing ourselves*."[15]

This kind of trial refers to the grand cycle of forgiveness—confession, repentance, penance, a vow to change ourselves and, at the end, the renewal of forgiveness. That is how the cycle is designed to work.

Yet many times that design does *not* work. The terrible and unanswered question behind Yom Kippur, and behind the very idea of forgiveness, is what do we do when there is no recognition of wrongdoing—a refusal even to acknowledge what happened, much less repent for it and change? What are we to do—people who have experienced terrible abuse and still have deep wounds that fester and burn?

There's not much lack of clarity in the gospels about our obligation to forgive. In Matthew, the Gospel reading for today, Peter asks Jesus how many times he should forgive someone: seven times? No, Jesus replies, seventy times seven times (which is symbolism for "an infinite number of times"). Also from Matthew come these pronouncements: "If anyone slaps you on the right cheek, turn to him the other also." And, "If you forgive others their sins, you will be forgiven. But if you do not forgive others, neither shall you be forgiven."

Was Jesus simply speaking hyperbolically? I don't think so. I think he saw forgiveness as an endlessly large bucket.

It is a difficult thing to stand here and tell Jesus that his teachings are inadequate to the needs of millions of his people, but that

15. Rabbi Dr. Reuven Hammer, "The 10 Days of Repentance," *My Jewish Learning*, https://www.myjewishlearning.com/article/the-ten-days-of-repentance. Emphasis added.

is what I have to say. I suspect these words have never been adequate at any point in history.

Too often our religion and our culture put the brunt of reconciliation on the wounded, making too few demands of the wounder.

I am thinking of physically, mentally, or spiritually abused children; the beaten spouses; those devastatingly damaged by family, friends, colleagues, or acquaintances. In certain churches, pastoral leadership piles hurt upon hurt, telling abused women, for example, that they must go back to their spouse and must forgive them. Many of the wounded have tried to reach out, hoping for reconciliation, but have been rebuffed. My first, smiley-face sermon does not even come close to meeting the needs of these children of God.

What are we to do? I will point to three things.

First, we must help the abused set some limits. One abused woman writes, "I don't know how many times I have turned the other cheek, only to get hit more each time. When do I decide that I have to protect my body and my soul?"

A twelfth-century Jewish philosopher, Maimonides, set forth some guidelines for repentance, speaking from the side of the transgressors who are seeking forgiveness from those they harmed. The wounder shall make three earnest attempts at apology, showing repentance as well as evidence that they have transformed. If, however, after the third attempt they are still rebuffed by the wounded, then the transgression now belongs to the wounded for withholding forgiveness.[16]

I will adapt this as follows: If the wounded person makes three attempts to connect and ask for recognition of the sin . . . ask the person to plead for repentance . . . and the person refuses, then the sin belongs totally and utterly to the transgressor. And thus the wounded person can proceed without guilt—often with the help

16. Maimonides, quoted in Maria Popova, "Repentance, Repair, and What True Forgiveness Takes: Lessons from Maimonides for the Modern World," *The Marginalian*, October 24, 2022. https://www.themarginalian.org/2022/10/24/repentance-repair-ruttenberg/.

of counseling or therapy— to move toward the kind of forgiveness we could better call, "letting go." You have done all you can do. Let go of it. Unburden yourself of your hurt and your guilt. As a wise counselor once said to me, if reconciliation is not an option, then can you at least give the hurt up to the light? Or throw it deep into the sea?

Second, we need to stop preaching and teaching forgiveness only in a way that puts the entire burden on the abused person. We must not add abuse on top of abuse. Yes, those who have been wronged have an obligation to open their hearts, at least for a time, to reconciliation. But we cannot demand seventy-times seven all the time from those who have been dangerously abused, whether physically, mentally, or spiritually. We cannot let those hearts be hurt again and again and again and again and again.

Finally, we must support people and organizations looking to help the severely abused: phone banks, shelters, halfway houses, mental health centers. These can be, quite literally, a lifeline. We must participate more openly in a community of care for the abused and must not simply give them easy words that actually put them more at risk. When it comes to forgiveness, we must be, as in Matthew 10, both innocent as doves and crafty as serpents.

I know that this second sermon is less likely to result in a smile and a friendly handshake on the way out today. Forgiving and asking for forgiveness can be joyful, but can also be grim, requiring much more strength than we might have presumed. We must be able to respond.

Let us hope for the first sermon, but also be prepared for the second one.

Our God, give us strength to seek both forgiveness and repentance in their many forms and manifestations.

Amen.

NOVEMBER

Wisdom

"Jesus or John?"

S.CAROLVS
BORROMEVS
Israel ex.
4.
9
Noue.

Wisdom:
"Jesus or John?"

Matt 6: 2–8

So when you give to the needy, do not announce it with trumpets, as the hypocrites do in the synagogues and on the streets, to be honored by others. Truly I tell you, they have received their reward in full. But when you give to the needy, do not let your left hand know what your right hand is doing, so that your giving may be in secret. Then your Father, who sees what is done in secret, will reward you. And when you pray, do not be like the hypocrites, for they love to pray standing in the synagogues and on the street corners to be seen by others. Truly I tell you, they have received their reward in full. But when you pray, go into your room, close the door and pray to your Father, who is unseen. (NRSV)

I *am going to set the stage here* with Jesus's baptism by John in the Gospel of Matthew, chapter three. Many of you are familiar with the story.

John the Baptist arises in the wilderness of Judea, baptizing and preaching. "Repent," he says, "for the kingdom of heaven has come near." John is drawing huge crowds, and gaining lots of fame. But the writer of Matthew tells the story of John as someone who is not the star of the show.

In John's dialogue, he says "After me comes one who is more powerful than I, whose sandals I am not worthy to carry. I baptize you with water but he will baptize you with the Holy Spirit and fire." Indeed, when Jesus comes to John to be baptized, John tries to deter him, saying, "I need to be baptized by you, so why are you coming to me?"

It is a lot of hemming and hawing to make the point that John wasn't the real deal; Jesus was. I'm not worthy, says John; I am preparing the way, showing the way. John points the way; Jesus *is* the way. How do we understand the Jesuses and Johns in our lives today?

Jesus or John? The names are not moral rankings, but existential roles. Most people in spiritual or creative leadership today are striving to be heard—but maybe we've misunderstood what true spiritual power looks like.

Johns are announcers, the louder ones out there, purporting to speak the truth, but who actually are merely pointing the way. They have online newsletters, blogs, podcasts, video channels, but all with the goal of getting more clicks and followers. They are only pointing the way. When Johns give to the needy, they announce it with trumpets. When they pray, they stand in the synagogues and on the street corners to be seen by others.

Jesuses offer something totally different. They are presence-bearers—quietly disruptive and incarnational. They don't have YouTube channels or TikTok accounts, or any other social media. No blogging, no newspaper columns. Nothing. The only power they have is in direct communion—reaching one person, or maybe hundreds. Direct interaction with people. Talking, listening, touching. An interaction of their spirit with others'. They do not point to the truth. In their own quiet way, they *embody* the truth. When they give to the needy, it is in secret; when they pray they go into their rooms and shut the door.

Jesuses are quieter, wiser, more likely to be non-judgmental and accepting, though not afraid to name dangers, quiet ones or loud ones. Able to smooth tempers, able to help people find common ground. In a sense, they are healers—not straight-up physical healing, but a healing of our souls. An encounter with a Jesus can be very brief. A salesperson, perhaps, or someone we meet walking the dog. They are not the preacher on a soap box, but maybe just an artist painting something along a canal or river, and chatting with people when they stop by. It is often not in the direct experience, but in our reflection afterward, that we realize we have just encountered a Jesus.

Who are the Johns you recognize in your life and who are the Jesuses? It is an important question because answering it can help you prevent yourself from being hurt or taken advantage of.

I knew a Jesus one time. I will call her Ruth. She was my mother's best friend from the time they were both in college. Through the ups and downs of my own family, she was a steadfast presence. She reacted not with judgment but with kindness and understanding—with a forgiving nature. Everyone was accepted, everyone was reclaimable. She never told you what to do, but you could feel her force within your soul leading to insights and knowledge that arose within you. She taught without teaching.

I have also known plenty of Johns. Let me give you one example of someone whose work I came to know quite well some years back. He was an extremely influential self-help teacher and motivational speaker who gave highly attended talks around the country and on TV.

For all his power and fame, though, he was a John driven by a very large ego. He was like many in spiritual, creative, or political leadership today who are striving to be heard, to gain power. But maybe we've misunderstood what true power looks like.

John draws a crowd with his voice. Jesus draws people with his life. John goes to the desert *to be seen*. Jesus goes to the desert *to disappear.*

Leadership in this technological age is overwhelmingly "John-shaped": mediated, performative, analytics-driven. It is primarily about clicks, page views, and followers. Notice me, notice me. Then, finally, pay me, pay me.

At times, Johns can be brilliant and courageous. At their best, their ability to point the way can be essential. More often, though, all the Johns create a cacophony of competing voices and egos. They become bewildering.

Instead, we can look for people who do not merely publish truth but embody it. Their wisdom can be found not in the clamor of the world, but in the quiet spaces of their hearts and our hearts. They help us listen and discern. They are a presence, not a platform.

With the great power of a successful John comes many responsibilities. Always remember that there is a third category of people—those struggling to make sense of the world, but who are neither Jesus nor John. They are the anxious, the bullied, the hungry, the oppressed, those with unfulfilled dreams, those in what they feel is a dead-end career or even a dead-end life. A poet once wrote about how many among us are just desperately trying to get by; our lives are silently despairing.

I fear that's true. Johns must be careful, for these people may be weak and fragile. They may be caught up in the quicksand of self-help books or different kinds of retreats and online groups. These people deserve our best thinking.

The danger is that the silently despairing may be more susceptible to the call of the false Johns out there—some Johns promising inner peace or enlightenment; other Johns offering riches, success, and timeshare contracts. Magic potions. Politicians who speak as if they are serving the people, but who are only interested in amassing power and riches. The world doesn't just need more voices. It needs more presences. Less amplification, more incarnation.

Friends, the question is not whether we will meet Johns and Jesuses in our lives—we already have. We can enjoy Jesuses—and Johns, too, as long as we keep our wits about us. One additional question, though, is: *Which will we become?* Will we spend our energy only amplifying our own noise, or will we risk becoming a presence of grace, of mercy, and of quiet power in a world that craves it? The world is aching not for more signs, but for the reality of God among us. So let us go, not as broadcasters of our own brilliance, but as bearers of Jesus's presence—in secret, in simplicity, and in love.

Our God, let us be aware of both the Johns and Jesuses in our life, and to take what is best from each of them.

Amen.

DECEMBER

FAITH

"Trust as the Foundation of All That Is"

S. SABBAS
ABB.
Israel ex.
5.
Decem.

Faith:
"Trust as the Foundation of All That Is"

Matt 9:20–22

Just then a woman who had been subject to bleeding for twelve years came up behind him and touched the edge of his cloak. She said to herself, "If I only touch his cloak, I will be healed." Jesus turned and saw her. "Take heart, daughter," he said, "your faith has healed you." And the woman was healed at that moment. (NRSV)

Heb 11: 1–3

Now faith is the assurance of things hoped for, the conviction of things not seen. Indeed, by faith our ancestors received approval. By faith we understand that the worlds were prepared by the word of God, so that what is seen was made from things that are not visible. (NRSV)

Rom 3:20–24; 27–28

For no human will be justified before him by deeds prescribed by the law, for through the law comes the knowledge of sin. But now, apart from the law, the righteousness of God has been disclosed and is attested by the Law and the Prophets, the righteousness of God through the faith of Jesus Christ for all who believe. For there is no distinction, since all have sinned and fall short of the glory of God; they are now justified by his grace as a gift. . . . Then what becomes of boasting? It is excluded. Through what kind of law? That of works? No, rather through the law of faith. For we hold that a person is justified by faith apart from works prescribed by the law. (NRSV)

We come to this last sermon of the year which takes place, actually, at the *beginning* of the church year—Advent and Christmas. It is a good time to reflect on the essence of things, which is faith itself. What is our faith? How do we describe it? How do we live it?

Throughout, I am going to refer to three arm gestures as a way to explain what faith is all about. Let's do them together.

The first is arms crossed tightly across our chest.

The second gesture is opening our arms, as if we're about to hug someone dear to us.

The third involves clenching our fists and churning back and forth, as if running a race.

Let's begin with arms crossed.

It's interesting to note that the first generation of Jesus-followers, the early Christian church, had no clear word for "faith" as in, a body of doctrines and practices: "the Christian *faith*." How could they, really, in those chaotic years when even Peter and Paul were fighting with each other?

What they did have was a word for what Jesus had taught them about the right way to think about living with God and with each other. How are we supposed to think about God? And then how is that supposed to inform what we say we believe and what we do to live within God's will?

The Greek word is *pistis*, often translated as faith, but which is really closer to the concept of "trust," or "trustworthiness," or "faithfulness." So in the Gospel of Mark, for example, when Jesus tells his disciples to have *pistis* in God, he is asking them to trust in God when they pray. When Paul speaks of God's *pistis*, as in one of the readings for today, he is referring to God's trustworthiness in fulfilling the promises made to us. The phrase, "God is faithful," means that we can trust God.

I like this emphasis on trust very much. Why? Because trust implies a necessary attitude or orientation for our lives. If we're not careful, the word "faith" becomes a wall of doctrine and belief that we retreat behind. It's like our arms crossed tightly against us. Think of your body language when you cross your arms: stay away. "This is my faith, and I'm not budging. I'm not going to be open to new ideas; I'm not going to read or learn anything outside of this faith of mine."

This is my concern about certain strains of conservative Christianity, as well as some other religions. Their arms are crossed. They think, "Those who don't believe exactly what I and my closed community believe are not saved." This attitude is dangerous to their souls and dangerous to the world.

Now let's move to arms open. By contrast, relying on trust as a central concept opens up our arms. We stretch them wide open to receive love—from people, from our communities, from the world, and from God.

I also like substituting "trust" for "faith" sometimes because it alters our interpretation of key biblical passages. Consider the Gospel story for today. A woman who has suffered an illness for many years reaches out to touch Jesus's cloak, believing that might heal her. And indeed, it does. Then consider what our new interpretation of the word "faith" does to this story. Jesus replied, "Take heart, daughter. Your *trust* has healed you."

How awesome was this concept of trust to Jesus and the developing church? Very. To illustrate, let's do a small amount of biblical analysis together. I promise it won't get too far down in the weeds.

What I want to do is spend some time with the verse from the epistle to the Hebrews that was read. Please follow along in the bulletin if you would like.

The verse begins, "Faith is the assurance of things hoped for, the conviction of things not seen." Based on the discussion we just had, we can immediately give it an alternative reading, which is, "*Trust* is the assurance of things hoped for."

Either way, it sounds profound, doesn't it, though I don't know about you, but I find it hard to understand. So let's look at it.

First, what's going on with the word "assurance"? It sounds kind of weak and passive to me. As it turns out, it's nowhere close to the power of the original meaning. The Greek word, "hypostasis," actually means something very grandiose: "the foundation of reality." That is, the foundation of our world and our lives. So it's really saying that trust is the foundation of what we believe.

Second, the word, "conviction" in the next phrase would more accurately be translated as something like, "proof." "Conviction" is OK, though it's a bit too "arms closed" for my taste. "Proof" is stronger, as in a proof of a theorem or proof that something exists. Either way, it refers to something strongly and deeply held. Trust enables us to have that proof or conviction.

Third and finally, what about this phrase, "things not seen"? What is that all about? It's actually part of the character of God. We do not and cannot see God, but we can see God's effects and activities; we have to trust that those things come from God. Like the cliché (though a true one) that we cannot see the wind, but we can see the trees swaying because of it.

There is a belief in Christian tradition that faith is not truly faith unless it is rooted in the unseen. St. Augustine wrote that hope isn't hope if its object is seen. The Nicene Creed recited by Christians everywhere begins with a belief in God, maker of heaven and earth, of all things visible and invisible—that is, both seen and unseen.

In a more secular way, art and literature act similarly. Writer James Baldwin once wrote in an essay on the creative process that "society must accept some things as real; but [the creative person] must always know that visible reality hides a deeper one, and that all our action and achievement rest on things unseen."[17]

If you rely only on the material world, on things you can see, you're probably going to miss some pretty important things happening around you that you cannot see.

17. Baldwin, "The Creative Process," *The Price of the Ticket*, 117.

When we add this all up, we get a new reading of the verse from Hebrews, which is closer to: "*Trust is the very foundation of everything we hope for, and the proof that what we cannot see is real.*" Trust—opening our arms, not holding them tightly to our chest—is the foundation of our lives.

Finally, there is the gesture of arms churning. This is another gesture that Christian scripture warns against. It is when we clench our fists and make our arms churn and churn, running, running, trying so hard to gain recognition, advancement, riches, love, worthiness . . . trying to prove something. It's never enough. But we don't need to prove anything to God. In our reading from Paul today, he tells us that we are not proven to be worthy by anything we *do*, including deeds based on the laws found in the Hebrew Bible.

Instead, since all of us have sinned and fall short of the glory of God, we are justified or made worthy by God's free gift of grace—*God's free gift of grace*—not by anything we could do or have done. We are justified by trust—trusting in grace, apart from works prescribed by the religious laws. This was, you may know, the basis of Martin Luther's ministry and writing, as well as other leaders of the Protestant Reformation.

The free gift of grace awaits us, but we cannot receive it until we open our arms. We don't need to close up and protect ourselves. We don't need to exhaust ourselves with endless churning after some goal.

What we need instead is to open our arms and trust. The gift awaits us, and it is free.

Our God, help us learn how to trust in you—how to receive your free gift of grace.

Amen.

About the Author

Craig Mindrum is the author of *Gardener of Peace* (2023) and *A Kind of Light: Joseph Conrad, Ethics, Literature* (1994). He did his masters work at Yale Divinity School and Indiana University (MA) then received his doctorate at the University of Chicago Divinity School. He taught in the religious studies department at DePaul University, Chicago. He has divided his career between writing, teaching, and business consulting.

Bibliography

Arendt, Hannah. *The Human Condition*. Chicago: University of Chicago Press, 1958.

Baldwin, James. *The Price of the Ticket: Collected Nonfiction, 1948-1985*. New York: St. Martin's Press, 1985.

The Book of Confessions. Office of the General Assembly of the Presbyterian Church (USA), 2016.

Brueggemann, Walter. *The Collected Sermons of Walter Brueggemann*. Louisville: Westminster John Knox, 2011.

hooks, bell. *Teaching Community: A Pedagogy of Hope*. New York: Routledge, 2003.

King, Jr., Martin Luther. *Strength to Love*. Boston: Beacon Press, 1981.

Lewis, C.S. *Surprised by Joy*. New York: Harcourt Brace and Company, 1956.

Nussbaum, Martha C. *Creating Capabilities: The Human Development Approach*. Boston: Belknap Press, 2011.

Sanders, E.P., *The Historical Figure of Jesus*. London: Allen Lane | The Penguin Press, 1993.

Whyte, David. *Consolations: The Solace, Nourishment and Underlying Meaning of Everyday Words*. Edinburgh, Scotland: Canongate Books, 2019.